BOB

BY PATRICK HUMPHRIES

Copyright © 1995 Omnibus Press (A Division of Book Sales Limited)

Edited by Johnny Rogan & Chris Charlesworth
Cover & Book designed by 4i Limited
Picture research by Nikki Russell

ISBN 0.7119.4868.2 Order No: OP47764

Exclusive Distributors
Book Sales Limited, 8/9 Frith Street, London W1V 5TZ, UK.
Music Sales Corporation, 257 Park Avenue South, New York, NY 10010, USA.
Music Sales Pty Limited, 120 Rothschild Avenue, Rosebery, NSW 2018, Australia.

To the Music Trade only
Music Sales Limited, 8/9 Frith Street, London W1V 5TZ, UK.

Photo credits:
Front & back cover: LFI. All other pictures courtesy of LFI, Barry Plummer, Harry Goodwin & Rex Features.

Every effort has been made to trace the copyright holders of the photographs in this book but one or
two were unreachable. We would be grateful if the photographers concerned would contact us.

Printed in Great Britain by Printwise (Haverhill) Limited.

A catalogue record for this book is available from the British Library.

OMNIBUS PRESS
LONDON · NEW YORK · SYDNEY

CONTENTS

INTRODUCTION

Bob Dylan has reached into the life of everyone with even a passing interest in popular music. Even those who hate Bob Dylan – those smoky, obfuscating lyrics, that booby-trapped voice – owe a debt to Bob Dylan. It is a cliché but, without Bob Dylan, pop would be a duller, emptier place. Without Dylan, no obvious 'new Dylans', no Randy Newman, Tom Waits, Paul Simon or John Prine. No Bruce Springsteen. There would have been no groups singing anything more than "Love ya, baby". No Sex Pistols, Oasis, Guns n'Roses or Led Zeppelin.

Dylan was a creature of his times. No pop star could ever have the same impact again. Singlehandedly, he gave popular music a voice, freed it from the inane shackles which bound it from when Elvis went into the Army until The Beatles arrived. Dylan refused to play by any rules. He re-routed rock between 1962 and 1968. He did it his way. Anything after that was a bonus.

Of all the Icons left over from the Sixties, he is really the only one still touring after all these years. A Dylan performance today is fraught and confrontational, a see-saw between the unforgettable and the inexplicable. For too long, Dylan has been toting his reputation round with him like a millstone. Coming fresh to this mad old man today, kids can't see what the fuss is about. In these days of multi-disc, self-program systems, you can skip over the dull bits. You might edit out the dreariness, but you also miss the drama. These days, what you get from Bob Dylan In Concert is King Lear: "Blow, winds, and crack your cheeks! Rage! Blow! You cataracts and hurricanes spout..."

Significantly, Bob Dylan has never gone through the door marked 'Easy Option'. In our lifetime we have seen Protest Bob, Electric Bob, Country Bob, Crooning Bob, Gospel Bob. For 30 years, news of a new Bob Dylan album could mean anything. If you're lucky it might be desolate landscapes, haunted by smoky, elusive imagery, or then again, it could be *Under The Red Sky*. Dylan can drive you to distraction, or break your heart with a ballad that sounds like it comes from before time. He has given so much that we have no right to expect any more; but more is what he wants to give, and we'd be crazy to refuse the offer.

Where Bob Dylan has been, can be traced from the records he has left behind. Often, he has moved on before we have had time to assimilate and appreciate them fully. Occasionally he has overstayed his welcome. Less frequently, he has failed to deliver. But always he has promised more.

Much has been written about Bob Dylan and even more has been speculated. In a career as wide-ranging, mercurial, frustrating and elevating as Dylan's, you could match a book this size to every one of his albums. Dylan's career, and the extraordinary times he lived through – and influenced – are landmarked by his official albums. That, in itself, can be a source of frustration, for much of what is considered to be Dylan's best material has never officially appeared on disc. Although, to be fair, Dylan's back catalogue has latterly been ably served by box sets such as *Biograph* and, particularly, *The Bootleg Series*.

Predictably, Dylan's determination to look over his shoulder – *Under The Red Sky* has been his only album of original material this decade – has upset the same fans who for so long crowed that there was no acknowledgement of his past. In a life woven through with myth and legend, it is by following Dylan's albums, like a thread connecting all the frustrating and confusing elements of his life, that we perhaps gain the clearest picture.

From his earliest interviews, Dylan successfully obscured his past. A ramblin', rollin' minstrel boy, bouncing between orphanages and carnivals, was obviously more appealing than the truth. The eldest son of immigrant Minnesota ironmongers, Robert Allen Zimmerman was brought into the world, 22" long and a buoyant 7lb 13oz, on May 24, 1941. An uneventful adolescence had Bob bowled over by Elvis. He witnessed Buddy Holly's last show, at the Duluth Armory. Dylan was a dyed-in-the-wool rock 'n' roller; his first original song was titled 'Hey Little Richard'. The teenage groups of his childhood Hibbing home were such decidedly un-folk combos as The Shadow Blasters and The Rock Boppers.

Having dipped into the obligatory Kerouac and Salinger in his late teens, Dylan subsequently discovered the lonesome folk of Odetta, the plaintive country of Jimmie Rodgers and Hank Williams and the keening delta blues of Robert Johnson. But it was hobo poet Woody Guthrie who the young Zimmerman locked onto. Reading Guthrie's autobiography *Bound For Glory* turned the restless singer's eyes to horizons way beyond Hibbing. In 1959, the 18 year-old Bob Zimmerman quit the iron ore town for the University Of Minnesota in Minneapolis. Eschewing his middle-class background, denying his Jewishness, Robert Zimmerman dropped out of university after less than a year, and made the journey to New York, where he arrived one snowy morning at the end of January, 1961. Which is where the story of 'Bob Dylan' really begins...

BOB DYLAN

RELEASED: JUNE 1962. CURRENT ISSUE: CBS CD 32001

Turned down by Vanguard, Folkways and Elektra Records, Bob Dylan signed to Columbia in October 1961. The label had no real foothold in the pop or folk marketplace, and was still coasting on its successes from Fifties' Broadway show albums and Mitch Miller singalongs. It was the determination of Columbia A&R executive John Hammond and the championing of *New York Times*' journalist Robert Shelton which led to Dylan signing to the label.

Bob Shelton's role in Dylan's career has too often been treated as a footnote. It was, after all, Shelton who 'discovered' Dylan. It was Shelton who went along to see Dylan supporting John Lee Hooker at Gerde's Folk City – rare enough for any critic to bother to see the support act. It was Shelton who saw that elusive *something* in the faltering, derivative 20-year-old's performance. And out of all the other 'Sons Of Woody Guthrie' around at the time, it was Dylan who Shelton fingered.

Dylan's eponymous début album contained 13 songs, which were recorded at a cost of $402 over two days during November 1961. Dylan's actual recording début had been as back-up harmonica player on Harry Belafonte's 1962 album *Midnight Special*.

Now venerated as rock's most accomplished songwriter, it is timely to reflect that on his début album, there are only two original Bob Dylan compositions – 'Talking New York', an inferior song to 'Hard Times In York' which surfaced 30 years later on *The Bootleg Series*, and 'Song To Woody'. The remaining songs were a reflection of Dylan's set list since his arrival in New York.

On the evidence presented here, it is hard to credit Shelton's eulogistic sleeve notes in which he says, Dylan is going "straight up". Dylan draws on blues, gospel, folk and pop – the opening guitar figure of 'Highway 51' borrows from the Everly Brothers' 'Wake Up Little Susie' for example. Celebrated as the great 'folk' singer, there is as yet precious little evidence of Dylan's folk roots.

The album provided a framework for much that followed: The Animals' 1964 'House Of The Rising Sun' acknowledged Dylan's version, and the Newcastle group's first single, 'Baby Let Me Follow You Down' also came from this source. Simon & Garfunkel turned 'Pretty Peggy-O' into a saccharine feast on their 1964 début, while in 1975, Led Zeppelin stretched the spiritual 'In My Time Of Dyin'' to over 10 minutes on *Physical Graffiti*.

What remains astonishing about Dylan's début is the maturity of the voice, which is hard to reconcile with the fresh-faced figure on the album cover. Dylan sounds like a 'Man Of Constant Sorrow', even though he was barely out of his teens. At an age when life and the future are usually paramount, Dylan already sings of what has been, and of ever-present death.

Dylan filched the melodies of his own early compositions from traditional folk ballads, which is where his later typecasting as a 'folk' singer would come from. But in his early incarnation, he was, in his own words, a "Woody Guthrie jukebox". Tapes in circulation from 1961 evidence Dylan covering Guthrie songs such as 'This Land Is Your Land', 'Pastures Of Plenty', 'I Ain't Got No Home' and 'Car Car'.

It is appropriate that the first of Dylan's compositions to attract wider attention was the homage to his mentor, 'Song To Woody'. Fumbling and faltering, it is undeniably sincere and was chosen by Dylan to open his set at the lavish 30th Anniversary Celebration held for him by his record company in New York in 1992. It was also the song which President Jimmy Carter chose to quote during his Inaugural address in 1977.

Dylan was frustrated by the five-month delay between recording his début album and its release: "I wasn't even me. I was still learning language then. I was writing then, but what I was writing I was still scared to sing".

What he was writing would change the face of popular music. A convergence of quiet questions would find Dylan irrevocably tied in to the burgeoning Civil Rights movement. 'Blowin' In The Wind' would always bring to mind the idealism which flourished in the days of the Kennedy Presidency, before that optimism was blown away in Dallas in November 1963.

THE FREEWHEELIN'
BOB DYLAN

THE FREEWHEELIN'
BOB DYLAN

RELEASED: NOVEMBER 1963. CURRENT ISSUE: CBS CD 32390

Sessions for Dylan's second album began on April 24, 1962, and ran on into the spring of 1963. One of the songs cut was Dylan's first single, the swiftly-deleted, rockabilly 'Mixed-Up Confusion' which, had it been made more widely available, might have pre-empted the fuss over Dylan's 'defection' to electric folk four years later.

Songs were pouring out of the 21-year-old Bob Dylan. He was going so fast that he couldn't keep up with himself, and his name was being mentioned in all the right places. Folk music needed its own James Dean, and Dylan fitted the image. Improbably, the image was matched by the quality of his songs, particularly one which Dylan wrote early in 1962, in a café on MacDougal Street, in Greenwich Village.

It is hard now to recall the impact of 'Blowin' In The Wind' on audiences in 1962: viewed from the 1990s, the nine questions posed by Dylan seem bland and rather naïve. Back then, on the journey towards Kennedy's New Frontier, 'Blowin' In The Wind' seemed to suggest answers rather than simply posing questions.

With hindsight, it is the line "How many years can some people exist before they're allowed to be free?" which lends the song its impact. There was never any question just who those "people" were.

In a world which sees the Civil Rights movement traduced to a "sight-gag" in *Forrest Gump*, it is worthwhile to recall just how important Dylan's song was to 'The Movement'. Thanks to Peter, Paul & Mary's hit single, 'Blowin' In The Wind' helped to galvanise a generation into action. Asking questions like "how many deaths will it take?" in the immediate aftermath of the Cuban Missile Crisis, gave the song an urgent topical spin.

So familiar was 'Blowin' In The Wind', that by the time Dylan came to release his own version of the song, he was tempted to leave it off his second album. Indeed, the complicated recording history of *Freewheelin'* has latterly seen a rare early version of it enter the record books as the most valuable pop album ever made.

The original *Freewheelin'* contained four 'lost' songs – 'Let Me Die In My Footsteps', 'Rocks & Gravel', 'Talkin' John Birch Society Blues' and 'Ramblin' Gamblin' Willie'. A stereo copy of this version would now be worth approximately £10,000. Reasons why the running order was changed for the official release are legion – Dylan's own dissatisfaction; Columbia's unhappiness at the 'John Birch' song... More likely, it was the fact that, at the time, Dylan was churning out songs on an almost daily basis, and preferred, say, his own 'Girl From The North Country' to the blues-weary cover of 'Rocks & Gravel'.

Freewheelin' is undeniably the album which properly marked the arrival of Bob Dylan as a potent new talent: popular music had never heard anything as antagonistic as 'Masters Of War', or as wide-ranging as 'A Hard Rain's A-Gonna Fall'. Bobby Vinton never sang of a world where "the executioner's face is always well hidden"; Bobby Vee's romances were not of the "gave-her-my-heart-but-she-wanted-my-soul" variety.

Love songs had never sounded as sincere or devout as when Dylan sang 'Girl From The North Country', nor vanquished childhood memories ever more remote than on 'Bob Dylan's Dream'. It is worth listening again to the timeless 'Masters Of War', and hearing the way Dylan lays into the faceless mercenaries. Rarely has a long-playing record contained such venom.

'A Hard Rain's A-Gonna Fall' was written in the aftermath of the 1962 Cuban Missile Crisis. This was the nearest the superpowers ever came to nuclear confrontation; the young and untested President Kennedy versus the scheming, belligerent Russian Premier Kruschev. "It was eyeball to eyeball," said Kennedy's Secretary Of State, Dean Rusk, "and the other fellow just blinked". Dylan's song is a litany of doom and disaster, a Brueghel vision of a world teetering on the brink of Armageddon. More, even than 'Blowin' In The Wind', 'Hard Rain' marked the emergence of that distinctive new voice which Shelton had first sensed barely a year before.

That same threat of extinction hung over the album's best satire, 'Talkin' World War III Blues', which took pot-shots at everything from nuclear paranoia to the triteness of Top 40 pop.

There was a coruscating edge, even on a song like 'Don't Think Twice, It's All Right'. It may sound unsettling for younger, present day listeners (only Dylan's time is considered at all "precious"), but back in less politically correct times, any song which tackled relationships at a level beyond "Love ya, again, baby" was to be welcomed.

It was as much the quantity as the quality of Dylan's songs which characterised that extra-ordinarily prolific burst, between 1962 and 1966.

In truth, *Freewheelin'* sits uneasily between castigating, "finger-pointing" songs ('Blowin' In The Wind', 'Masters Of War', 'Hard Rain') and the frivolous ('Talkin' World War III Blues', 'Bob Dylan's Blues'). Humour was always an integral part of the Dylan arsenal, but too many of the songs here are one-take, one-gag ideas, which jarred alongside the detailed, studied merit of, say, 'Bob Dylan's Dream'. The final track, 'I Shall Be Free', allowed the young Dylan to fantasise about a world of fame and wealth which, within weeks of the album's release, would be his for the asking.

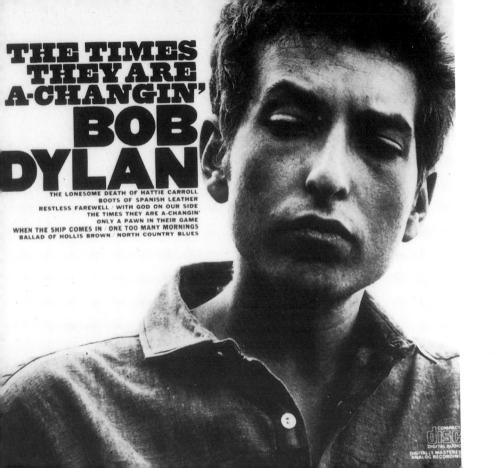

THE TIMES THEY ARE A-CHANGIN'

RELEASED: MAY 1964. CURRENT ISSUE: CBS CD32021.

Dylan's third album was as stark and ascetic, as black and white, as its cover implied. The levity of *Freewheelin'* now firmly replaced by dour wisdom. If anything, Dylan sounded even older and more bitter here.

For all its success at rallying and drawing attention to inequality, 'Blowin' In The Wind' had sounded dreamily abstract. 'The Times They Are A-Changin'' was sharply focused protest, with Dylan as castigator, cracking an accusatory whip. "Don't criticise what you can't understand" is a great get-out line, and helped the song become the universal clarion call of disaffected youth.

'The Times They Are A-Changin'' was written just prior to Kennedy's assassination in Dallas. It is a song which brings together all the elements of buoyancy and optimism that the Sixties seemed to offer. But for all the song's modernity, its challenging of established values, its recognition of the generation gap, the tone is defiantly Old Testament. The song, delivered in Dylan's best sackcloth and ashes voice, perfect-

ly suited to the medieval tone of the language and its apocalyptic imagery. Of the song, which came to be an anthem for the Sixties, its title endlessly recycled in subsequent newspaper headlines, Dylan said: "I wanted to write a big song, some kind of theme song, with short, concise verses that piled up on each other in a hypnotic way". He did.

But the album had more to offer than just its title song. 'When The Ship Comes In' is equally impressive. In hindsight, much of the optimism and promise that the Sixties offered, and which Dylan articulated, is to be found in this song. Maybe because 'The Times They Are A-Changin'' has become such an anthem, it can now seem almost as much of a cliché as the ideas that Dylan set out to destroy. 'When The Ship Comes In' is less well known, and carries more impact when dreaming of the bright shining future, which was dealt such a bloody body blow in Dealey Plaza on November 22, 1963.

This was to be Dylan's last album of specifically protest songs. During his two-year professional career, Dylan had already written dozens of songs (few of which ever made it onto official recordings) about specific incidents of intolerance and injustice – 'The Ballad Of Donald White', 'Who Killed Davey Moore?', 'Death Of Emmett Till'.

Dylan had become the articulate figurehead of a movement. He was the designated heir to Woody Guthrie, he had the approval of the Old Left and the adulation of the impressionable young. Dylan was making 'folk' and 'protest' sexy. Tom Paxton, Phil Ochs, David Blue, Eric Andersen, Joan Baez, Judy Collins, Tim Rose, Tom Rush, Paul Simon, Peter, Paul & Mary... all of them were reading the same books, getting indignant about the same issues, going on the same marches. But it was 22-year-old Bob Dylan who best expressed the anger and articulated the dreams and aspirations of his generation.

'The Times They Are A-Changin'' proved to be Dylan's protest swansong. Although he would bring the same indignant fire to flame in later years on 'George Jackson' and 'Hurricane', 'The Times They Are A-Changin'' was the last time Dylan could be accused of writing to order. 'With God On Our Side' was nothing less than a history of America, its nine verses balancing guilt and responsibility. The God whom Dylan addresses here is the vengeful God of the Old Testament, not the warmly embracing Deity revealed on parts of *Slow Train Coming*.

'The Ballad Of Hollis Brown' was based on a newspaper account. While described as a 'ballad', its repetitive verse structure is blues-based. Like a grainy black and white film, Dylan's unembellished story tells of relentless suffering and pointless death. The final line offers not a smidgen of hope as the story weaves its cycle.

In a similar style was 'North Country Blues', a bleak evocation of a community ground down by economic hardship, and the price a small town has to pay when the work dries up. Similar in tone to Elvis Costello's 'Shipbuilding', 'North Country Blues' conveys Dylan's sympathy for the underdog, and is an excellent example of his eye for detail, which stops even his most blatant "message" songs becoming mere propaganda.

'Only A Pawn In Their Game' again drew on newspaper reports, but rather than stridently protesting at the racist murder of Medgar Evers, Dylan pulls back and looks at the whole rotten business of racism. Pre-empting Gene Hackman's character in *Mississippi Burning*, 'Only A Pawn In Their Game' has the maturity to recognise that the poor white trash are as much victims of the system as the vilified blacks.

'The Lonesome Death Of Hattie Carroll' drew on the real-life murder of black maid Hattie Carroll by white socialite William Zanzinger. Dylan's indignation rises when Zanzinger is convicted of murder but receives only a six-month sentence: 26 weeks for taking a human life. "Now", rails Dylan, "is the time for your tears".

The remaining songs on *The Times They Are A-Changin'* aren't exactly laugh-fests either. 'One Too Many Mornings' is a fiery, poetic memory of a splintered love affair. The restlessness found there also finds root in the autobiographical 'Boots Of Spanish Leather', one of Dylan's most eloquent and melodic love songs. Drawing on bitter personal experience, the song creates its own bobbing and weaving atmosphere. It fixes a moment in time, the sense of loss and desolation evoked by the line: "The same thing I want today, I will want again tomorrow".

Dylan claimed 'Restless Farewell' was written to swell out the album. Fans have long since identified its weary tone of resignation with the composer's own desire to be moving on, and no longer bound by the expectations of his audience. The final line, about bidding farewell and not giving a damn, was a hint of the arrogance to come, as Dylan's star continued to rise and he found his audience expanding. It had been one hell of a ride.

Just as *The Times They Are A-Changin'* was making its initial impact, The Beatles stopped being a British novelty, and took the first steps towards becoming an international phenomenon. Dylan found something he could identify with in The Beatles' irresistible harmonies; just as he savoured The Animals' taking acoustic folk songs and surging electricity, The Searchers' beguiling 12-string guitars and gentle folk protest, and The Rolling Stones' championing of black R&B.

At heart a diehard rock 'n' roller, he had found himself increasingly pigeonholed as a solitary folknik. But with his 'protest' duties discharged on 'Blowin' In The Wind' and 'The Times They Are A-Changin', it was time for Dylan himself to be changing.

Another side of Bob Dylan

ANOTHER SIDE OF BOB DYLAN

RELEASED: AUGUST 1964. CURRENT ISSUE: CDCBS 32034

The 11 songs for Dylan's fourth album were recorded in one extraordinary, red wine-fuelled session, on June 9, 1964.

"There aren't any finger-pointing songs in here" Dylan told journalist Nat Hentoff immediately prior to the session. "Me, I don't want to write for people any more. You know – be a spokesman. From now on, I want to write from inside me".

"Inside" meant a move away from the panoramic, social issue songs which had dominated Dylan's last album. *Another Side Of...* is certainly a lighter load than *The Times They Are A-Changin'*, but it was seen by some as a betrayal of established 'authentic' roots. Dylan's 'defection' also had an impact on a personal level, a lot of those Leftists who had struggled through the Depression of the Thirties, a world war against fascism and the McCarthy witch-hunts of the Fifties, had invested a great deal of hope in Bob Dylan. As long as his songs were cut from the same cloth as Woody's, everything was fine. As soon as the boy went weird, he put a lot of

people's backs up.

The Times They Are A-Changin' had been an all-purpose protest album, perfect for capturing the mood of the times, but an album which has not worn well during the intervening years. While there is still dead wood on *Another Side Of...*, the album also contains some of Dylan's most ambitious lyrics, and displays him playing with the rhythms of songs such as the piano-pounding 'Black Crow Blues' and the 'Bob-As-Ben E. King' 'Spanish Harlem Incident'. Dylan was obviously keen to apply the electric sounds he had heard over in England, to his own music.

The levity is evident on the album's opening track, 'All I Really Want To Do'. Gone is the bitter anguish of 'Don't Think Twice' and 'Boots Of Spanish Leather'; all Bob wants here is to "baby, be friends with you". It is a song which has him playing with rhymes, as much for their sound as their meaning.

The album's main love song is both fluid and rich: 'To Ramona' is intimate and affecting, a flower of the city, Ramona lives and breathes. Intense and twisted, Dylan weaves a tapestry, a lurid depiction of a relationship, born out of desperation and desire. 'I Don't Believe You' is playful, clever and heartless, while 'It Ain't Me Babe' has Dylan as accuser once again – if the relationship has failed, it ain't his fault, babe.

Like Woody Allen at the same time, Dylan was placing his women underneath a pedestal. Nevertheless, there was a freshness and vivacity to these love songs that no one else was writing. They were also among the first songs in pop to examine the battleground of relationships. The most extreme example was the album's longest track, 'Ballad In Plain D'. Intensely autobiographical, the song was Dylan exorcising himself, a spiteful flashback to a failed relationship, doomed, thought Dylan, by an interfering elder sister.

'Ballad In Plain D' is an inordinately detailed, languorously melodic, account of Dylan's break-up with Suze Rotolo, the muse pictured alongside him on the cover of *Freewheelin'*. Suze had inspired all of Dylan's most moving love songs up until then. Later, Dylan had the good grace to admit: "That one I look back at and say, 'I must have been a real schmuck to write that'. Of all the songs I've written, maybe I could have left that alone".

On a lighter note, 'I Shall Be Free No. 10' has some good gags (the spoof Cassius Clay poetry, the "all the farms in Cuba" line, the monkey with a mind of its own...), while 'Motorpsycho Nitemare' sounds like it was recorded as much for the amusement of the onlookers in the studio as it was for Dylan's pleasure.

The album's two 'major works' were 'Chimes Of Freedom' and 'My Back Pages'. 'Chimes Of Freedom' is strong on atmosphere and deep in meaning. Ripe for interpretation, it was all too much to take at the time – don't forget, no Dylan album before *Empire Burlesque* in 1985 had lyrics printed on the sleeve. A good part of any Dylan fan's adolescence was spent with ear pressed against the Dansette, trying to figure out just what the hell he was singing.

Confronted with the torrent of images and allusions in a song like 'Chimes Of Freedom', you were left spellbound by the sheer vividness of the language. This was Dylan, moving on from the specifics of railing against the 'Masters Of War'; here was a poet let loose on a world of victims and underdogs. At times, it seemed like Bob Dylan was the only one able – or willing – to articulate on behalf of those that the system had ground beneath its boot.

The refrain of 'My Back Pages' gave Dylan another catch-phrase: "I was so much older then, I'm younger than that now". It is a song, like 'Restless Farewell,' which bids adieu to a part of the singer's life. It was hard to believe Dylan was barely 23 years old as he sang of his youth buckling beneath wisdom and experience.

Such was Dylan's impact at the time, that fledgling English folk-rock band Fairport Convention extracted a song ('Jack O'Diamonds') from the sleeve poems on *Another Side Of...*

Reluctantly, he was performing the songs people had paid to hear. Solo and acoustic, Dylan would stand stage centre and sing of injustice and inequality. But inside his head, "some other kinds of songs" were being heard. The "black and white" view of life the singer dismisses in 'My Back Pages' had already blurred into shades of grey. Tiring of the mouthpiece he had become, Dylan was soon to be slipping the shackles.

Dylan's fourth album proved to be a valediction. Critics thought they discerned the sound of someone moving away from his roots. *Another Side Of Bob Dylan* was, in fact, the faint echo of somebody already long gone.

Bob Dylan
Bringing It All Back Home

BRINGING IT ALL BACK HOME

RELEASED: MAY 1965. CURRENT ISSUE: CDCBS 32344

Dylan was hungry for crossover pop acceptance. None of his albums had cracked the American Top 20, and he watched enviously as The Beatles and the Stones shot ahead. But the prophet wasn't motivated by profit. If it had been hard cash, Dylan could have sat down and written production-line variations on songs which had already proved successful for him – 'The Times They Are A-Changin' Tango', 'Blowin' In The Wind Bossa-Nova'.

He was comfortably off. By the beginning of 1965, the cover versions of 'Blowin' In The Wind', 'It Ain't Me Babe' and 'Don't Think Twice, It's All Right' alone paid for comfortable out-of-town residences and holidays.

Dylan's reach was to exceed his grasp. He seemed driven to attain the impossible and, in 1965, he led rock 'n' roll into its most ambitious and extraordinary year since Elvis Presley first checked in at 'Heartbreak Hotel' a decade before. The ensuing 18 months witnessed the most substantial sequence of work ever undertaken by an American recording artist. *Bringing It All Back Home* may not sound like a revolutionary album today, but 30 years ago, it wasn't rock 'n' roll, it was heresy.

Dylan had long since favoured amalgamating styles and songs. A bootlace-tied rock 'n' roller at 13; a Hank Williams-style drifting cowboy from his late teens; a Woody Guthrie boomtown rat bound for glory by the age of 20. Folk hobo, iconoclast and innovator; by the time he came to record his fifth album, at the age of 23, Bob Dylan had already bounced around the great pinball machine of American popular music.

Reports of concerts immediately prior to that first electric flourish at Newport in July 1965, had Dylan clearly dissatisfied with the restrictions of solo acoustic performance. He was tiring of what was expected of him. He was getting off on what The Animals, The Beatles and the Stones were accomplishing. He wanted to pound the hammer on the anvil.

Dylan was chafing at the restrictions he felt imposed upon him as a solo performer. On its release in March 1965, diehard fans were assaulted by the electric rapping of 'Subterranean Homesick Blues', which gave Dylan his first American Top 40 hit. The song followed 'The Times They Are A- Changin'' into the British charts, separated by only a month. British fans were baffled by the shift from Biblical prophecy to handle-pilfering vandals.

The album opened with the in-your-face 'Subterranean Homesick Blues', which leaned heavily on Chuck Berry's 1956 'Too Much Monkey Business' (and was in turn, borrowed by Bruce Springsteen for 'Blinded By The Light', Elvis Costello on 'Pump It Up' and REM for 'It's The End Of The World As We Know It').

On record, Dylan's jump in 1965 was understandable. In concert, it was taken as treachery. Dylan went from flavour of the month to pariah. Coming fresh to it today, *Bringing It All Back Home* isn't as radical as you might expect from such a ground-breaking album: the electricity is muted, and the album's four major songs on side two were all strictly solo and acoustic. But heresy is never graded. *Bringing It All Back Home* was a slap in the face for the purists who had followed Dylan all the way from the coffee houses of Greenwich Village into the despised Top 10.

Bringing It All Back Home gave Dylan the commercial clout he desired, enough to put him on a level with The Beatles and the Stones. He was also cocky enough to know how good he was ("I could have written 'Satisfaction'," he told the Stones, "but you could never have written 'Tambourine Man'."). But Bob wanted more than serious, spotty students and big-boned girls in glasses following in his wake. He wanted the whole Carnaby Street- Mod- hip- cool-man style thing. He didn't want denim & sackcloth & ashes & talking 'bout a revolution.

Dylan called *Bringing It All Back Home* his first "three-dimensional" album. Certainly, it marked a further broadening of vision, a process begun on *Another Side Of Bob Dylan*. Leaving specific issues behind him, Dylan was peering at 'the system', and, on songs such as 'Subterranean Homesick Blues', 'Maggie's Farm', 'Gates Of Eden' and 'It's Alright Ma (I'm Only Bleeding)', was bitterly dismissive of what he found. 'Hollis Brown' and 'Hattie Carroll' were a long way behind. Roughly divided into dark and corrosive love songs and assaults upon the establishment, *Bringing It All Back Home* is still a bold and audacious album.

The album is a lexicon of Dylan catch-phrases

– "You don't need a weatherman to know which way the wind blows"; "Don't follow leaders"; "don't look back"; "There's no success like failure"; "Let me forget about today until tomorrow"; "He not busy being born"; "Crying like a fire in the sun"; "Money doesn't talk, it swears".

For all the new freedom his application of electricity offered Dylan, many of the songs still borrowed from familiar styles – 'Gates Of Eden' and 'It's Alright Ma...' solo acoustic in the 'folk style'; 'She Belongs To Me', 'Maggie's Farm', 'Outlaw Blues', 'On The Road Again' relying heavily on a blues structure.

'Maggie's Farm' would gain added currency 14 years later, on the election of Margaret Thatcher as Prime Minister, when three million jobless realised that they too would never work on Maggie's farm no more.

'She Belongs To Me' and 'Love Minus Zero/No Limit' are persuasive and poignant love songs. Even if the actual meaning is confusing – that "failure is no success at all" is observing the bleeding obvious. No matter, Dylan still swept you along, simply on the strength of his language, the vividness of his images and the intensity of his performance.

Down the years, the songs still resonate. 'Mr Tambourine Man' remains one of Dylan's greatest-ever songs, all the more regrettable that The Byrds' better-known version, a number one hit on both sides of the Atlantic in the summer of 1965, is such a sad, truncated travesty. Steeped in mystery and imagination, Dylan's 'Mr Tambourine Man' stands as proof positive of his ability, if not as poet, then certainly as a supreme blender of words. The last verse, particularly, has all the resonance and quality one would normally associate with a 'great work' – disappearing through "the smoke rings of my mind", and off on a journey at times reminiscent of Jean Cocteau's *Orphée,* but also evoking images from cinema, poster art and literature, the listener is brought back again and again by Dylan's magnificently weary chorus.

By Dylan's own admission, 'Mr Tambourine Man' is the only one of his songs that he ever tried to write "another one" of. Although weighing in at over five minutes, there is a tautness and discipline to 'Mr Tambourine Man' which is sorely lacking in the subsequent two songs on the album.

'Gates Of Eden' presents a landscape

populated by caricature grotesques – cowboy angels, shoeless hunters, "Utopian hermit monks", "motorcycle black Madonnas", "grey-flannel dwarfs"... all in a relentless procession, leading nowhere, while the hapless listener must scrabble "into the ditch of what each one means".

'It's Alright Ma (I'm Only Bleeding)' fares better, with Dylan casting his caustic and coruscating eye on a bankrupt society. Morally and emotionally stultified, the world Dylan bears witness to here, is a world gone wrong. It is a song of curious topicality – at the height of Watergate, with an embattled Richard Nixon fighting for his political life, the biggest cheer on Dylan's 1974 tour was reserved for the line: "Even the President of the United States sometimes must have to stand naked".

Twenty years later, a different kind of topicality attached itself to the line "Advertising signs they con you..." as Dylan licensed the use of 'The Times They Are A-Changin'' for a 1994 TV commercial promoting a firm of financial consultants.

Throughout this album though, Dylan sang with intensity and conviction, and even if you had a job catching the words, you couldn't help but be moved by the performance of a song like 'It's All Over Now, Baby Blue', the work's dignified closing song. Almost in anticipation of what lay ahead, the song acts as a valediction to the Bob Dylan that was. He has struck another match, he has started afresh and, for those who cannot move forward with him, it really is all over now.

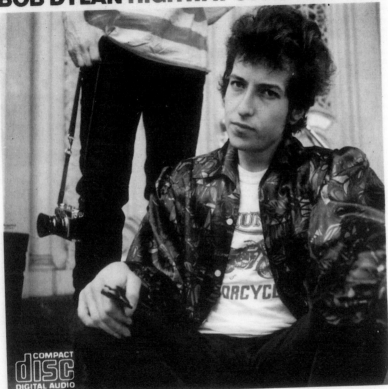

BOB DYLAN HIGHWAY 61 REVISITED

HIGHWAY 61 REVISITED

RELEASED: AUGUST 1965. CURRENT ISSUE: CDCBS62572

Barely drawing breath, Dylan unleashed what many, myself included, regard as the finest rock album ever made. Looking back from the vantage point of the mid-Nineties, when rock has become such an industry, what Dylan achieved during those few fertile months seems even more miraculous. Today, the release of an album is synchronised worldwide, to ensure that the six or so singles lifted from it will each have their videos aired in turn, enticing the purchase of the CD, DCC or Mini-Disc. A 'UK tour' has become a week at Wembley or Earl's Court, with 'The Act' brought to you, courtesy of Volkswagen or Pepsi.

Things were a little bit different 30 years ago. Pop still provided a real focus, fans were loyal to acts. Back then, there weren't any monthly music magazines or MTV; hell, there wasn't even any legitimate UK pop radio. Albums were the conduit to your favourite act, an LP sleeve was a decent size and the purchase of an album allowed you access to a closed world.

The sleeve of *Bringing It All Back Home* was a treat. It let you have a glimpse into the private world of Bob Dylan: Bob cradling a cat (named, significantly we later learned, 'Rolling Stone'; a languid woman in red (Bob in drag cried the gossips!), an album by (who the hell?) Robert Johnson... And four years later, wasn't the sleeve of *Nashville Skyline* familiar from that Eric Von Schmidt album pictured on *Bringing It All Back Home*?

The sleeve of *Highway 61 Revisited* was a disappointment, just Bob in a motorcycle T-shirt, but once you got inside...

'Like A Rolling Stone' was already familiar as a single. It had given Dylan his biggest American hit, only kept off the number 1 slot by Sonny & Cher's 'I Got You Babe'. But *Highway 61 Revisited* was an album of many centres. Almost precisely a year earlier, The Animals' 'House Of The Rising Sun' (itself owing a minor debt to Dylan) had shattered the previously inviolate hold of the three-minute pop single. 'Like A Rolling Stone' took it all one step beyond, while the album's closing track, the 11-minute 'Desolation Row', just took rock stratospheric.

Much has been made of 'folk-rock'. Dylan was undeniably its leading exponent and by the time of *Highway 61 Revisited*, he had honed his craft. Taking stories and narratives from the folk and ballad tradition, Dylan fused his lyrics with the driving rock rhythms that he had relished from his youth.

Dylan's earliest rock roots had been invigorated by his exposure to The Beatles and The Rolling Stones. It was no mere coincidence that he titled his fifth album – the first to be released after the British Invasion had made its impact – *Bringing It All Back Home*; paying homage to the beat groups who had rekindled interest in the native American rock 'n' roll of Buddy Holly, Chuck Berry, Eddie Cochran; the intense R&B of Muddy Waters, Rufus Thomas and the seamless pop of Berry Gordy's burgeoning Tamla Motown empire.

On *Another Side Of...*, Dylan was already abandoning straightforward narrative. By the time he reached *Highway 61 Revisited*, he was

off on a whole other journey. The album began with the words made comfortingly familiar by every nursery tale: "Once upon a time...", then proceeded off on its own wayward, whirlwind path. Distilled from a far longer work (40 pages Dylan estimated at one time), 'Like A Rolling Stone' was Dylan at his most venomous and lacerating, it is one of rock's great put-downs (along with its contemporary single, 'Positively 4th Street').

At its end, after four weaving and unforgettable verses, after a chorus that somehow seemed to catch the craziness and mayhem of the mid-Sixties, when that first post-war generation was looking for a direction home, or away; Dylan's sneering, rasping, discordant questions on 'Like A Rolling Stone' seemed almost perfectly in tune with the times.

The genesis of the song, like so many of Dylan's, is dubious: he and Bob Neuwirth are seen singing Hank Williams' 'Lost Highway' (which begins with the singer describing himself as a rolling stone) in the film *Don't Look Back*. The young Bob Zimmerman would certainly have been familiar with Muddy Waters' 1950 'Rolling Stone' – the song from which Brian Jones took the name of his R&B group. While the 'rolling stone' which gathered no moss had been in circulation since the 16th Century. Written while Dylan was holed-up in Woodstock, road-weary from his 1965 UK tour, the composer later admitted that 'Like A Rolling Stone' "started with that 'La Bamba' riff".

'Tombstone Blues' was funny, one of those production-line surrealist slices Dylan could seemingly turn out in his sleep. They're all there – blues singer Ma Rainey nuzzles up to Beethoven, alongside John The Baptist, Cecil B de Mille, Galileo and Jack the Ripper. For all its frivolity, Dylan at least sounds like he's having fun with the song, and while there may not be much in the way of lasting merit, 'Tombstone Blues' at least reminds us that Dylan was never po-faced about his work and could enjoy a good joke. A word too for Mike Bloomfield's searing guitar, which so enhances the whole album.

Nobody ever had the gall to ask Dylan to explain why 'It Takes A Lot To Laugh, It Takes A Train To Cry'. As an album filler, the song displayed Dylan's tiredness of touring, and its refrain gave Steely Dan a title for their début album. Dylan returned to the song when he was touring during 1991, hammering it into a jagged, electric Chicago southside blues.

'Ballad Of A Thin Man' features high in the canon for many Dylanologists. I've never been convinced by its flimsy merits. There are enough memorable lines, but then Dylan was too capable a writer to let any song of the period go by without at least one striking vignette or image. The intense feelings of paranoia and persecution are diluted by clumsy images which Dylan bought as a job-lot during 1965 and a cast which is all too familiar (one-eyed midgets, lumberjacks, cows etc). The refrain that "something is happening here, but YOU don't know what it is, do you...?" found favour with those, who only a few years before, had castigated parents for criticising what they couldn't understand.

By this stage of his career, Dylan was too astute to let the song slip out of his hands. He is in control on 'Ballad Of A Thin Man', but aside from the striking chorus, the song has not weathered well.

'Queen Jane Approximately' on the other hand, is one of those undervalued songs of the period. There is a weariness, a sense of regret and unrealised commitment here. Dylan sends out a message of desperation from somewhere on the road. Another song, fashioned somewhere in England, 'Queen Jane Approximately' is muddy and allows the listener to be left wanting. Ever helpful, Dylan told journalist Nora Ephron (later to achieve distinction as a film director with *Sleepless In Seattle*) in 1965: "Queen Jane is a man".

Highway 61 ran from Dylan's boyhood home of Duluth, way down South, along the spine of the nation. Although a powerful symbol, the title track itself was a throwaway. Again, you sense Dylan had more fun making it than we do listening to it. It is a crisp rewriting of one of the Old Testament's most haunting tales: Abraham being asked to sacrifice his son to prove his devotion to God. The same tale inspired Leonard Cohen's chilling, 1968 'Story Of Isaac'. In Dylan's hands, there is slightly less reverence: when asked by the Supreme Deity for his son's blood, Abraham replies "Man, you must be puttin' me on". Dylan enjoys the song, plays the numbers game (40,000 shoe strings, a thousand telephones, the fifth daughter on the twelfth night...) then blows out of town. It is a song Dylan frequently returns to in performance, and for all its frivolity, has maintained its place in fans' affections.

'Just Like Tom Thumb's Blues' has all that road-weariness contained in its jaundiced performance. Dylan sounds like he is singing through a fog, and there were enough references to stimulants to confirm what everyone thought at the time. Dylan sings of not having the strength to "get up and take another shot"; someone looking fine on arrival, leaves "looking just like a ghost"; and finally Dylan singing that he started out on red wine, before hitting "the harder stuff". Following on from the "smoke-rings" of 'Mr Tambourine Man', 'Just Like Tom Thumb's Blues' sounded like Dylan wouldn't be around long enough to be hit by any backlash.

'Desolation Row' is plain, but far from simple, with Bob buzzed only by Bloomfield's jagged guitar. Nobody had ever made this kind of 11-minute odyssey in pop before. Dylan's world on 'Desolation Row' is powerfully post-apocalyptic. Whatever once was, has gone, disappeared in a blazing conflagration, leaving a world populated only by grotesques and travesties. Dylan is at fault when assembling his cast, his choice of characters is too random and none is given any flesh. Only

Cinderella can be visualised, with "her hands in her back pockets, Bette Davis style". Despite that, the impact of 'Desolation Row' is only reinforced by its snowballing effect.

'Desolation Row' meanders like a snake, all its despair and disillusion to be found in Dylan's world-weary reading. It doesn't end as it should though, with the sinking of the Titanic. As a symbol, the disastrous maiden voyage of the largest movable, man-made object on earth, on the eve of the First World War, takes some beating.

If Bob felt it worth namechecking Ezra Pound and T.S. Eliot, that was good enough reason for me to seek out 'The Love Song Of J. Alfred Prufrock', 'cos that had something about mermaids too. 'Desolation Row' also has Bob getting to the *Phantom Of The Opera* long before Lloyd Webber. With hindsight, 'Desolation Row' may have been weakened by its relentless juxtaposition of celebrities and myths – besides, everyone's done it since – but back then, when Dylan was the first kid on the block to try something that ambitious, 'Desolation Row' was a spray-can allegory, a grim fairy tale, a rock 'n' roll *Recherche Du Temps Perdu*.

Highway 61 Revisited didn't end there either. The sleeve notes had Dylan at his most caustic and confident, reading like he was a Graduate of the University of Amphetamines; Dylan's pun-fuelled nonsense was far removed from the bright and breezy cockiness of Beatle sleeves.

Dylan ended the liner notes for *Highway 61 Revisited* by writing: "you are lucky – you don't have to think about such things as eyes & rooftops & quazimodo". Bob did. He didn't have time to think about much else.

STEREO
Can Also Be Played In Mono

featuring I WANT YOU and

BLONDE ON BLONDE

RELEASED: AUGUST 1966. CURRENT ISSUE: CK 6447

With The Band on board, Dylan set off to terrorise the civilised world. Established as a bona-fide pop star, Dylan played nearly 50 shows between May and July 1966, but diehard Dylan fans still couldn't take the idea of their idol fronting a pop group; it seemed to them that Bob was debasing himself before the false gods of money and fame.

Only Dylan could inspire such devotion and provoke such feelings of betrayal. If you went to a concert by Cliff Richard, you didn't go to boo. Crispian St Peters never aroused such hostility in his fans. This was only the second generation of rock 'n' roll, the amplification in halls was primitive, achieving a sound balance was nigh-on impossible... but the over-riding feeling left by that incendiary 1966 concert tour was of betrayal.

Loyal fans who had stood by Bob and put up with all the disparaging comments (Can't sing for toffee, what are his songs about..?) went along and heard their hero drowned out by a pop group. Pop groups were Freddie & The Dreamers, not Bob Dylan and The Band. Guitarist Robbie Robertson recalled: "You get off the plane and play – people booed you. We thought 'Jesus, this is a strange way to make a living!'"

The head-on collision between Dylan and The Band has been one of rock's great mysteries. The reality is that a secretary in Dylan's manager's office took Bob out to see the boys somewhere in the swamps of New Jersey, sometime in 1965. In *Don't Look Back*, when asked why he had other musicians on his record, he smiles and says they're his friends "And I have to give my friends work, don't I?"

It's a theory Marianne Faithfull enthusiastically explored in her 1994 autobiography. She gives a compelling fly-on-the-wall account of Dylan at the height of his pop star adulation: "When he came back... with The Band... he was so happy... and it made you realise just what a drag it must have been being out there all by himself with an acoustic guitar, just moaning away. This was exacerbated by being in England, where all the musicians he was meeting were in groups... All that boys' club stuff that makes it so much easier."

Out on a limb, Dylan was also under pressure to deliver a novel – he couldn't let John Lennon be the only literary pop star. He was touring, his manager had committed him to a TV special, his contract with CBS was due to expire. And there was the question of that new album... The pressure was on. Begun in New York at the end of 1965, *Blonde On Blonde* was wrapped in Nashville by February 1966.

Nashville didn't have a skyline in 1966. Nashville was where Country & Western was diluted to taste, in studios light on atmosphere, but heavy on time-is-money. The Nashville Sound was lush, wraparound strings, drowning out any real emotion on production-line pop songs, which were only made 'Country' by virtue of a weeping steel guitar. It wasn't quite what Bob Dylan had in mind...

Blonde On Blonde is a dark and brooding collection. As rock 'n' roll's first double album, it beat Frank Zappa's *Freak Out* by a clear two months. Recorded with the cream of the Nashville session aces and a little help from "mathematical guitar genius" Robbie

Robertson, the album's 14 songs were quixotic examples of where Dylan's Medusa-like head was at during those punishing first months of 1966.

From the scowling, unfocused Bob on the cover, through to the 10-minute homage to his bride Sara on 'Sad-Eyed Lady Of The Lowlands', *Blonde On Blonde* just teems and overflows. The bulk of the songs were busked in the studio; Dylan only had shadows of what he wanted. His outlines were given flesh by the musicians, initially wary of the wiry-haired pop star, and a sort of camaraderie emerged in the Nashville bunker.

In the past, it had been relatively easy for Dylan to scat his way through an album, when there was only him, his guitar, harmonica and occasionally piano, to satisfy. With *Blonde On Blonde*, Dylan had to try and convey the sounds inside his mind not only to other musicians, but to session men with precious little *sympatico*. Remarkable then, that for Dylan, *Blonde On Blonde* came the "closest I ever got to the sound I hear in my mind... It's that thin, that wild mercury sound. It's metallic and bright gold..."

Touring though was taking its toll. Dylan

sounded as hazy on vinyl as he looked on the album cover. Hindsight again lends a different perspective on the album; knowing that it was to be his last original work for 18 months – a lifetime in rock 'n' roll back then – there seem all manner of omens and portents within *Blonde On Blonde*.

Some of Dylan's best work is to be found among the autumnal hues of *Blonde On Blonde*, but the relentless pressures of an increasingly successful career meant that, for the first time since his début, he was too busy to be original. He was now to be found borrowing from those he had previously left far behind. 'Fourth Time Around' is an engaging re-write of The Beatles' 'Norwegian Wood', which had appeared on *Rubber Soul* six months before, while 'Temporary Like Achilles' and 'Obviously 5 Believers' sounded like Bob Dylan trying to ape the Bob Dylan of a year before.

There is no real 'Country' on the first album by a rock star to be recorded in Nashville. 'I Want You', 'Rainy Day Women # 12 & 35', 'Leopard-Skin Pill-Box Hat' were lightweight pop, although the refrain "Everybody must get stoned" (from 'Rainy Day Women...') found easy favour at the time.

'Stuck Inside Of Mobile With The Memphis Blues Again' was another of those great Dylan songs about places. Few American songwriters have conveyed the space and variety of their nation as well as Dylan, the poet of the place-name. He manages to convey the full awfulness of being marooned in Mobile, Alabama burning with the blues from Memphis, Tennessee. It doesn't mean a lot, but with a talent as blazing as Dylan's, his vagueness is frequently far more satisfying than the precision of others.

'Just Like A Woman' is a song with English overtones and images (fog, royalty, pearls), and one which sits uneasily on today's ears, with its litany of selfish, sexist slurs. Of its time though, its smoky melancholy slots neatly into the weary and resigned world Dylan created in *Blonde On Blonde*.

'Most Likely You Go Your Way (And I'll Go Mine)' and 'Absolutely Sweet Marie' rock along best without much scrutiny (surely, if you live outside the law, you are, perforce, dishonest?). There is the usual, utility cast of Dylan characters – Persian drunks, guilty undertakers, neon madmen and the Queen of

Spades. Bowled along by the composer's relentlessness, much of Dylan's stuff at this time was swallowed without scrutiny.

At his best though, he could carry you along on the strength of his performance and the conviction of his lyrics. The magnificently wasted 'One Of Us Must Know (Sooner Or Later)', is a bitter farewell played out against desolate landscapes beneath glowering, leaden skies. However, the whole side devoted to 'Sad-Eyed Lady Of The Lowlands' suggested Dylan was out-reaching his grasp. 'Desolation Row' was longer and still managed to squeeze three more songs alongside it, on Side 2 of *Highway 61 Revisited*.

Of all Dylan's atmospheric songs of the period, 'Sad-Eyed Lady...' weaves its own world around Dylan, sounding as world-weary as Humphrey Bogart in the neon-lit Rick's Bar in *Casablanca,* as Ilsa quits him, again. There is a lot of puff here (What, please is a "geranium kiss"? Describe a "cowboy mouth") but there is also a rolling hymn of devotion with some extraordinarily intense commitments and pledges contained therein.

The masterpiece of the set is 'Visions Of Johanna'. A New York song cut in Nashville –

that estrangement lends atmosphere to the work. The first verse is perhaps Dylan's finest evocation of time and place. Wide-ranging and ubiquitous, 'Visions Of Johanna' switches from a clammy attic room to a courtroom where Infinity is judged; from empty parking lots on West 4th Street to a no-show Madonna, prowling an empty cage.

A mournful harmonica plays, a drug-induced nightmare follows halfway through the fourth verse: women with faces like jelly and missing knees, a donkey standing draped with "jewels and binoculars" (an image The Rolling Stones would borrow three years later for the cover of *Get Your Ya-Yas Out*).

'Visions Of Johanna' has Dylan sounding wise as leader, old as Time. Few have attempted cover versions of this impossibly convoluted song. At his iconoclastic best, Dylan explains Mona Lisa's inscrutable, enigmatic smile as a bad case of the "highway blues", but there aren't many laughs to be had here. This is mystery and imagination, with an organ playing skeleton keys in the wispy background, and near the end, Dylan's conscience explodes, and he is gone, while all that remains are his 'Visions Of Johanna', ambiguous and dazzling images which he has entertained over a lifetime.

The summer of 1966 saw The Beatles unleash *Revolver,* their most mature album to date. The Beach Boys' *Pet Sounds* sounded like the only American album to tackle the Fabs head-on. Dylan's manager Albert Grossman had scheduled 60 more concerts for the remainder of the year, significantly including a date at Shea Stadium. The Beatles had played the New York baseball stadium the previous year, establishing a record for the largest ever attendance at a pop concert. Grossman was now determined to put Dylan on a commercial par with The Beatles.

Dylan had established a base at the artists' community of Woodstock, north of New York. It was while riding his motorcycle around the muddy, tree-lined paths of Woodstock that the back wheel on Dylan's machine locked, and he was hurled over the handlebars.

The few people who had been close to Dylan in the weeks before the crash remarked on the singer's ghost-like pallor. You could hear how weary he sounded on record and in interview. There was a tragic inevitability to the crash, the legend of James Dean loomed large. Youth needed another martyr.

Dylan's legendary status was enhanced by the crash, marking as it did a period of withdrawal, when the only stories to emerge from Dylan's Woodstock retreat were rumours. As pop convulsed during the Summer of 1967, Bob Dylan sat far away in upstate New York, looking out at the trees and staring at the sky.

BOB DYLAN
JOHN WESLEY HARDING

JOHN WESLEY HARDING

RELEASED: FEBRUARY 1968. CURRENT ISSUE: CDCBS 4633592

The album for which the word 'inscrutable' might have been invented. The last the world had heard of Bob Dylan was as a corkscrew-haired mystic, smokily seeing the world through his warehouse eyes. Since Dylan's motorcycle crash of July 1966, there had, of course, been rumours. Those in the know (usually the older brother of a friend) knew someone who said that Dylan was horribly disfigured in a hospital; that his "bike crash" was a euphemism for a drugs overdose; that the CIA had had him 'taken out'; that he had been recording with The Band in the basement of a house distinctively, if ungrammatically, known as 'Big Pink'. They also said, "If you were Jonathan King or Manfred Mann, you could get to hear those songs".

Whatever the truth, Dylan's absence was remarkable. Never before had a rock star of his stature endured such a withdrawal from the public eye – Elvis's two years in the Army had been tempered by Colonel Parker's systematic releasing of stockpiled material. All that the world had heard from Dylan was a workmanlike *Greatest Hits* in March 1967 (see final chapter). After five years, we all knew where Bob Dylan had been, what we wanted to know was where he was going.

The first the world got to hear of the 'new' Bob Dylan was the strumming of a single acoustic guitar and the story of a kindly and misunderstood chap, who happened to share the same name as a wicked outlaw. Played out against a curiously lightweight, C&W-tinged backing, Dylan told his tale in three short verses, and was gone. Only one song out of the 12 contained on *John Wesley Harding* differed from the strict three verse structure. It was a long, long way from the haunted cityscapes of 'Visions Of Johanna'.

The almost staccato simplicity of the new material was, however, deceptive. There were hidden depths to songs such as 'The Wicked Messenger': in anyone else's hands, a throwaway, two minute album filler, but transformed by Dylan into a rich and enigmatic variation on the 'kill the messenger' theme. The uplifting 'Drifter's Escape' has a Franz Kafka hero set on a bass-heavy collision with Hank Williams' hillbilly alter-ego, 'Luke The Drifter'.

'The Ballad Of Frankie Lee & Judas Priest' was long and tortuous, just the sort of epic which Dylan fans relish sinking their teeth into. After allowing listeners to make up their own minds about whether the song's big, bright house was a church or a brothel, Dylan helpfully concluded the song by underlining its moral.

It would take the whirlwind electric magic of Jimi Hendrix to bring out the real menace of 'All Along The Watchtower'; but where Hendrix's was a Technicolor glimpse of impending Apocalypse, Dylan's original was low-key, black and white, and in its own way equally disturbing.

Despite his undoubted wealth and long-time absence from 'the street', Dylan showed that he still sided with the underdog on songs such as 'I Am A Lonesome Hobo' and 'I Pity The Poor Immigrant'.

The album's final two songs, 'Down Along The Cove' and, especially 'I'll Be Your Baby Tonight', were signposts on the way to *Nashville Skyline* – both sweet-sounding Country songs, highlighted by the quintessential pedal steel of Pete Drake.

It wasn't just the voice which sounded different either: Dylan had undergone another one of his physical transformations. The Polaroid cover had a neighbour, three Bauls of Bengal and ol' Bob squinting into the sun, beneath a wide-brimmed hat and wispy beard. It was the first time he'd smiled on an album cover since 1963. The sleeve notes helpfully advised that "the key is Frank".

An open Bible lay in Dylan's Woodstock study during his exile, and the language of the King James edition permeates what Dylan called the "first Biblical rock album". In length and scope, only 'The Ballad Of Frankie Lee & Judas Priest' recalled what had gone before. This was a wiser, older Dylan, advising you to help your neighbour, and not go mistaking the sublime for something near at hand.

In retrospect, *John Wesley Harding* stands as one of Dylan's richest and most rewarding albums, providing its fair share of coinage: "Nothing is revealed", "he was never known to make a foolish move", "There must be some way out of here", "If you cannot bring good news, then don't bring any" ...

But what people wanted at the time was something sympathetic to the times – Bob Dylan's *Sgt Pepper*. Wisely, or conveniently, Dylan had ducked below the parapet during the turbulent upheavals of 1967, and had not felt the need to compete. In fact, *John Wesley Harding* pioneered a trend both The Rolling Stones' and Beatles' albums of 1968 (*Beggars Banquet* and *The Beatles*) marked as a return to roots.

On the surface, *John Wesley Harding* was deceptively slight and superficial, but it has worn well. The album's best songs are either of innocents despoiled ('Drifter's Escape', 'I Pity The Poor Immigrant', 'Dear Landlord') or evoke a tugging, turbulent world of the Old Testament ('All Along The Watchtower', 'I Dreamed I Saw St Augustine', 'Wicked Messenger'). At its best, *John Wesley Harding* displays Dylan's disciplined writing, sheared of the excesses which made his pre-crash work so impenetrable. As it is, *John Wesley Harding* reveals further riches with each play and, despite its stark instrumentation and teasing lack of pretension, probably stands as Dylan's most mysterious album.

Having recorded two albums on the trot in Nashville, it should have come as no surprise (particularly bearing in the mind the crooning Country of *John Wesley Harding*'s final track, 'I'll Be Your Baby Tonight') when Dylan fully immersed himself in the big muddy which was Country & Western. Bob Dylan may have been ready, but the world was far from prepared for such a sea change.

NASHVILLE SKYLINE

RELEASED: APRIL 1969. CURRENT ISSUE: CCDCBS 63601

Dylan had made no secret of his love of Country & Western music. Hank Williams, Hank Snow and Johnny Cash had long been favourites, while Cash was an early – and influential – supporter of Dylan's at Columbia.

If The Byrds' 1968 *Sweetheart Of The Rodeo* was the original 'Country-Rock' album, coming nine months before *Nashville Skyline*, it was Dylan's approbation which kickstarted the genre.

Nashville Skyline is an album which still divides Dylan purists. Listening to it now, it is hard to grasp just what a seismographic impact it made on its release. Looking back though, you can appreciate the concern for Dylan's future which the album prompted: Dylan's duet with Johnny Cash on the album's opening track, 'Girl From The North Country', was the first time he had ever gone back to re-record one of his own songs; the album contained Dylan's first instrumental and, most significantly of all, the lyrics on *Nashville Skyline* seemed to epitomise the very "moon in June" slop which Dylan had singlehandedly destroyed five years before. The album

clocked in at under quarter of an hour a side. All in all, *Nashville Skyline* saw Bob Dylan made mortal for the first time in his career.

Of course, *Nashville Skyline* had much to enjoy, if not marvel at. Dylan had rarely sounded more relaxed on record. Pete Drake's weeping pedal steel guitar lends muscle. 'One More Night' is as jaunty and forceful as an Elvis song on Sun Records. 'Lay Lady Lay' is lilting and enticing, while 'Country Pie' is as effective a piece of nonsense as any piece of Country hokum.

The album gave Dylan his biggest ever hit single, 'Lay Lady Lay', which was written for the 1969 film *Midnight Cowboy*, although in the end Dylan missed the deadline, and Harry Nilsson's performance of 'Everybody's Talkin'' got the gig. Dylan also added a couple of lines to Roger McGuinn's 'The Ballad Of Easy Rider', for the 1969 film *Easy Rider*, but modestly chose not to be added to the credits.

Nashville Skyline revealed a new Bob Dylan. Here was a man who had wrenched love songs into the 20th Century and given us those heartfelt, tormented ballads, pining over the loss of "the only pal I had". Certainly, to hear the man who had entirely re-written the language of pop music, crooning "by golly, what more can I say" was quite shocking. Of *Nashville Skyline*, like Hollywood, there is no 'there' there. It is an album of Dylan demystifying himself, and in the process providing us with some charming songs – 'I Threw It All Away', 'One More Night' and that's about it.

Nashville Skyline could have been a far more substantial album, if any one of the other dozen or so Dylan-Cash duets had been included, if 'Wanted Man' (an excellent outlaw song Dylan had penned for Cash) had been included... but then the career of Bob Dylan is as full of 'ifs' as Kipling's poem.

If the world at large knew of the existence of *The Basement Tapes*, or that this was only to be the first of many Dylan write-offs, maybe *Nashville Skyline* would have been better received. As it was, the criticism was severe, but the real wrath was to be reserved for Dylan's first double album since *Blonde On Blonde*.

SELF PORTRAIT

RELEASED: JULY 1970. CURRENT ISSUE: COL 4601122

Dylan had straddled the 1960s like a Colossus. His first release of the 1970s boded ill. His limitations as a painter were obvious from the sleeve of The Band's 1968 *Music from Big Pink*, but he stuck with the palette, and as a title, *Self Portrait* sounded promising: Bob running through some Woody Guthrie, Leadbelly, Hank Williams and Little Richard songs which had inspired him as a lad. Well, actually, no...

Dylan was irked at being the victim of rock's first bootleg. *The Great White Wonder* in 1969 had collected together 1961 recordings and the best known of 1967's *Basement Tapes* on a double album, which went on to sell 250,000 copies in America without Dylan seeing a penny in royalties. For Dylan, *Self Portrait* was wilful self-destruction. In 1985, he recalled: "There was a lot of other stuff that was worse appearing on bootleg records. So I figured I'd put all this stuff together and put it out, my own bootleg record, so to speak... If it had actually been a bootleg record, people would probably have sneaked around to buy it".

At the time of the album's recording, Dylan was being harassed by A.J. Weberman, infamous 'garbologist' and founder of The Dylan Liberation Front, and Dylan's summer '69 appearance at the Isle of Wight Festival – his first pre-publicised live appearance in three years – had received poor reviews.

By the beginning of the Seventies, Dylan was under siege. He was tired of being the font of all teenage knowledge, he was weary of pilgrims trudging up to his Woodstock door and he wanted to let the pressure off. *Self Portrait* was his own bootleg, an attempt to demystify the voice of a generation by showing that he had feet of clay.

Self Portrait didn't so much demystify Bob Dylan as nearly destroy him. The four live tracks from the Isle of Wight revealed the flimsiness of that performance, and had him mangling 'Like A Rolling Stone', arguably his greatest song. There was no Woody, but there was the curious sound of Bob Dylan singing 'Blue

Moon', and duetting with himself on Paul Simon's 'The Boxer', Dylan & Garfunkel?

In fact, once the furore had died down, *Self Portrait* threw up one or two gems. The album reinforced just what a powerful interpretative singer Dylan could be, as he tackled songs such as 'Copper Kettle' and 'Days Of 49'. And even Dylan at his most contrary couldn't butcher such well-structured songs as Gordon Lightfoot's 'Early Mornin' Rain' and The Everly Brothers' 'Take A Message To Mary'.

While his own new songs were lightweight, 'Belle Isle', 'Alberta' and 'Little Sadie' were fine if taken at face value as pop songs. There was some decidedly flimsy material, like 'Wigwam', 'All The Tired Horses', 'Woogie Boogie' and 'Minstrel Boy'. It was a real curate's egg of an album, which could have made an effective simple, single album. Indeed, one of the benefits of Compact Disc is editing and re-programming the 24 tracks of *Self Portrait* to make an enjoyable selection.

But at the time, and hard on the heels of the disappointing *Nashville Skyline, Self Portrait* was perceived as Bob Dylan's big kiss-off. Only six months into the Seventies and on this evidence, Dylan was relegated to the archive of the Sixties.

NEW MORNING

RELEASED: NOVEMBER 1970. CURRENT ISSUE: COLCD 32267.

If *Self Portrait* was unfairly dismissed, and could have been one hell of a single album, *New Morning* was a single album which had an undue amount of praise heaped upon it. Having survived the hysteria of the Sixties, now happily married and a father afresh, Dylan was keen to convey the tranquillity he had found. Driven to leave Duluth, determined to make it in New York, flung into the whirlwind of fame, the Sixties had been a merry-go-round, until the motor-cycle crash gave Dylan time to draw breath and gain perspective on a life that had seemed to be slipping away from him.

Ironically, the breath of fresh air presaged by *New Morning* had little to do with the clear, crisp mountain air of Woodstock. Dylan had moved his family back to live in New York during 1969. But woven through with memories of rural tranquillity, *New Morning* exudes an air of reflective contentment. The title track celebrates country streams and blue skies, and remains one of Dylan's most simple and affecting songs.

After years of searching and questing, 'Sign On The Window' finally recognises that parenthood "must be what it's all about". 'Time Passes Slowly' and 'Winterlude' are further evidence of Dylan's fondness for country pie, the latter sounding as cosy as a reel from a Frank Capra film.

The customary mystery was to be found on 'Went To See The Gypsy', an account of Dylan visiting Elvis Presley in concert in Las Vegas (Dylan had told *Rolling Stone* that Elvis's version of his own unreleased 'Tomorrow Is A Long Time' was his most treasured recording). 'Day Of The Locusts' was a vivid account of Dylan receiving an Honorary Doctorate from Princeton. The album ended with the hymnal 'Father Of Night', a devotion which was surely tongue in cheek, wasn't it?

New Morning was a good album, but not a great album – 'One More Weekend' is a leaden rocker, 'If Not For You' deserved to be a hit for Olivia Newton-John, while 'If Dogs Run Free' had Bob proving he could 'do' jazz, if he really wanted.

New Morning was an adequate stop-gap. It was not intended to be Bob Dylan's last album for nearly three years.

PAT GARRETT & BILLY THE KID

PAT GARRETT & BILLY THE KID

RELEASED: OCTOBER 1973. CURRENT ISSUE: COLCD 32098

The early Seventies threw up a slew of new heroes. There wasn't any need to rely on old contemptibles like The Beatles and Bob Dylan, not when you had Ziggy Stardust & The Spiders From Mars and Bruce Springsteen. But Dylan's absence only enhanced his myth. The years of silence – almost twice as long as the period between *Blonde On Blonde* and *John Wesley Harding* – saw a torrent of Dylan bootlegs, which kept the flame burning. Dylan's sporadic guest appearances included gigs and albums by Allen Ginsberg, John Prine, Leon Russell, Doug Sahm, Steve Goodman and David Blue. The highest accolade any aspiring singer-songwriter could hope for during those years of silence from the old Dylan, was to be referred to as a "new Dylan".

It was also the time when Dylan began to be revived by the literary establishment. His lyrics were seen to be a reflection of the turbulence and fluctuating fortunes of the Sixties, as well as applying a vivid and fresh language of the streets to the more formalised strictures of the written word.

It was a situation heightened by Michael Gray's excellent 1972 book *Song & Dance Man*, the first serious look at Dylan as poet. Its strength lay in recognising that, in Dylan's universe, Arthur Rimbaud and Eddie Cochran could contentedly co-exist.

The 'poet' tag was authorised by Dylan himself with the publication of *Writings & Drawings* in 1973, which gathered together for the first time all of Dylan's lyrics, so you could finally get to see what you had imagined hearing all those years.

While the man himself was away, Dylan's armour was pierced by the first full-length biography. Anthony Scaduto's *Bob Dylan* was published in 1971, and retains a cherished place in many Dylan fans' hearts as the first detailed squint behind the sunglasses which Dylan affected for the world.

It was all well and good, but what the world wanted was some new 'product' from Bob Dylan. There were, as ever, rumours, and all those "new Dylans" were occupying the press far more satisfactorily than any single old one could ever do.

Pat Garrett & Billy The Kid occupied Dylan for months on the dry and dusty Mexican border. There had been talk of Bob Dylan as an actor ever since he burst onto the scene a decade before, but wisely, he had avoided the mistake of diving straight into film. Robert Shelton reports the 20-year-old Dylan being particularly impressed by Elia Kazan's film *A Face In The Crowd*, a parable about a disingenuous folk singer who becomes a demagogue, thanks to the power of television. Although dated (to give you an idea of just how old it is, Walter Matthau plays the romantic lead) you can still see its appeal for the young singer. Offers had been dangled before Dylan, the most tempting had been to play Holden Caulfield in a – still unfilmed – version of J.D. Salinger's *Catcher In The Rye*.

The route of Pop Star As Actor was already littered with the corpses of those who'd died in the attempt – Elvis Presley, Cliff Richard, John Lennon, Mick Jagger – when, in 1973, Dylan accepted a subsidiary role in Sam Peckinpah's film, *Pat Garrett & Billy The Kid*.

Among the few pop stars to have successfully made the transition from vinyl to celluloid, was ironically, one of the better, early Seventies' "new Dylans", Kris Kristofferson, and it was he who approached Dylan to appear as 'Alias'.

Peckinpah's reputation had tumbled from the heights it reached following 1969's triumphant *The Wild Bunch*, and neither *Straw Dogs* nor *Junior Bonner* had achieved anything like its impact. It seemed, Peckinpah was happier back in the Old West. Kristofferson played Billy The Kid, James Coburn was a leathery Sheriff Pat Garrett, while Dylan hovered on the periphery.

Squinting and edgy, Dylan's performance is best remembered for the exchange: "What's your name boy?" "Alias." "Alias what?" "Alias anything you want"; and for the scene where he dons glasses and reads out the contents of a grocery store shelf. *A Streetcar Named Desire* this was not, but it was Dylan's sense and sensibility which saw him avoid the acting limelight, and settle instead for a shadowy support.

Despite a butchering at the hands of the studio, *Pat Garrett & Billy The Kid* remains one of Peckinpah's finest films, and Dylan's theme music is a perfect accompaniment to the director's vision. Because of the anticipation accorded Bob Dylan's first album of original material in nearly three years, the soundtrack album of *Pat Garrett & Billy The Kid* was a disappointment to many. True, there were only four vocal performances, and three of these were based around a single song, but returning to *Pat Garrett & Billy The Kid*, you are struck by the rightness of the music. The opening and closing themes perfectly capture the windswept and haunted landscapes of New Mexico, the soundtrack veering from buoyancy to tragedy.

The 'Billy' evoked by Dylan's three takes of the outlaw is a tragic figure, damned by destiny, and sure to be shot by a friend. Dylan wrings every sweaty ounce of emotion from each dusty, saddle-sore mile. As a writer, he was again transfixed and inspired by the place names in his songs – Boot Hill, Tularosa, Rio Pecos, San Pedro, Taos, El Paso... It's the same Catholic, border territory which would so memorably inspire 'Romance In Durango' two years later.

The three variations of 'Billy' captured on the album are each subtly different: 'Billy 1' is jaunty and scene-setting; 'Billy 4' is sprawling and pensive, while 'Billy 7' sounded like the bleary result of a tequila sundown. And while one song, however varied, may be stretching it over a whole album, there was a welcome joy in hearing Dylan sing again of outlaws outrunning the long arm of the law.

For all the slightness of the soundtrack album, *Pat Garrett & Billy The Kid* did boast Dylan's most successful post-Sixties' song, 'Knockin' On Heaven's Door'. First and unforgettably heard as Slim Pickens' Sheriff Baker sits and watches his dream boat slip away from his dying hands, the song went on to provide hits for Eric Clapton, Randy Crawford and Guns n' Roses. Ironic for a man renowned for the complexity and spiralling language of his 'rock poetry', that it should be the two verse, hymnal 'Knockin' On Heaven's Door' which brought Dylan's name to a whole new audience. But it is that very directness which makes it such an affecting song, and there remains something intensely moving in hearing Dylan handle the song, on a good night, in front of a devout crowd.

For all its calm and contemplative impact, 'Knockin' On Heaven's Door' is a dark and wilful song, and for Dylan, with *Pat Garrett & Billy The Kid* released to respectful reviews for his performance, there was still a "long black cloud" dogging him, in the shape of his record label.

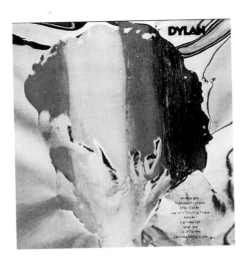

DYLAN (A FOOL SUCH AS I)

RELEASED: NOVEMBER 1973. CURRENT ISSUE: COLCD 32286

Recorded as studio warm-ups for *Self Portrait* in 1970, *Dylan* was little more than a loose collection of cover versions. It was rushed out as a spoiler by Columbia Records, the label Dylan had recorded with for a decade, his whole professional career. Mogul David Geffen had landed Dylan for his own fledgling Asylum label in 1973, and Columbia was mightily pissed off. While Dylan's record sales had never come close to those of The Beatles or Rolling Stones, he was undeniably a figurehead for any record label.

Widely regarded as the worst Dylan album ever, the man whose name was on the cover "didn't think it was that bad, really". Certainly, a selection of the best covers here ('Lily Of The West', the acoustic 'Spanish Is The Loving Tongue' from the B-side of 'Watching The River Flow', 'The Ballad Of Ira Hayes', the folk ballad 'Mary Ann') wouldn't have sounded inappropriate dotted on *Self Portrait*. As it was, *Dylan* had Bob sleepily tackling the Elvis hits 'Can't Help Falling In Love' and 'A Fool Such As I'.

Again, in retrospect, *Dylan* really wasn't that bad. What rankled at the time was that fans knew there were shelf-loads of vintage Dylan tapes gathering dust in Columbia's vaults, but instead of the fabled 'Farewell Angelina', they were fobbed off with Bob Dylan half-heartedly crooning Joni Mitchell's 'Big Yellow Taxi'.

At the time of the album's release in 1973, it seemed further evidence that Dylan's talent had dwindled throughout the Seventies. As many focal points of the Sixties were realising, standing your ground in rock 'n' roll's third decade was problematic. None of the solo Beatles' work came close to matching the sales of their work together, while The Rolling Stones were finding their legend steadily eclipsed by Led Zeppelin.

Except for the faith of his most diehard, committed fans, there had certainly been little to suggest that Dylan had anything fresh to offer the new decade. His influence had long ago permeated the body politic of pop and he had seen lesser talents hijack his style. But there was no evidence among his recent work that this inscrutable man, now entering his thirties, had anything substantial with which to appeal to the new musical generation.

Bob Dylan was not alone in finding that the Seventies had little but uncertainty on offer.

PLANET WAVES

RELEASED: JANUARY 1974. CURRENT ISSUE: CDCBS 32154

He still wasn't dropping the '& Drawings' bit on the job description. Dylan's cover illustration for his 13th album was the weakest thing on it. Incredibly, this was the first music to be credited officially to 'Bob Dylan & The Band' during their nearly 10 years together.

In a three-day session during November 1973, Dylan and The Band laid down the 10 songs which made up *Planet Waves* – 'Forever Young' was taken both fast and slow. Dylan sounded in charge, the swift recording process and sympathetic backing resulted in his most confident sounding album since *Blonde On Blonde*. He took the bulk of the songs at a clip, and on the album's two set pieces ('Dirge' and 'Wedding Song') was suitably funereal, wordy and mysterious.

The opening track 'On A Night Like This', recalled the homely values espoused on *New Morning*. 'Going, Going, Gone', 'Hazel', 'Something There Is About You' and 'Never Say Goodbye' (which also featured the return of 'Baby Blue') further evoke a fondly imagined, rural Arcadia; a safe world of childhood, from which to dream of all the potential and possibilities which lay ahead once you've flown the coop.

At the time, 'Forever Young' sounded like Dylan's tongue was firmly in his cheek. Back with The Band, sounding confrontational, hitting the road hard and emerging from the shadows, a song hoping for righteousness and demanding a strong foundation for faith seemed at odds with the Dylan currently on display. Reminiscent of 'Father Of Night' on *New Morning*, this had to be a put-on, hadn't it? But much had changed, besides hair-length and trouser-width, since the Sixties. Written for one of his children, 'Forever Young' was simple, sincere and devotional, when people still expected multi-faceted complexity from Dylan.

On *Planet Waves*, Dylan recorded 'Forever Young' twice: as a slow, stately end to the first half of the album, and at a faster pace for the opening of the second half. For many years, the song remained a staunch concert-closing favourite, either that or 'Knockin' On Heaven's Door' was sure to get the Zippos and Swan Vestas out and waving in unison. But that belies the simple, direct appeal of the song, of a father's wishes for his children; of certainty and devotion in a world fuelled by uncertainty and faithlessness.

Critics hovered like vultures over the album's two most lyrically accomplished compositions.'Dirge' inevitably set tongues wagging about the state of Dylan's marriage - "I hate myself for loving you..." wasn't the most enticing opening line to a love song, but Dylan's detours down Suicide Road and Lower Broadway sounded promising. If the song was wrung from inner, heartfelt turmoil, if it was endeavouring to construct something tangible out of the abstracts of relationships, then the inclusion of the line "in this age of fibreglass, I'm searching for a gem" was a dirty, rotten shame.

The other side of the coin was on 'Wedding Song', intense and heartfelt, but this time about the true love, the acme of womanhood, the wife. This Dylan was a long way removed from the self-centred man of 'It Ain't Me Babe' or 'Just Like A Woman'; this was desperation born out of deep love. More autobiography was apparent as the singer denied it had ever been his intention to "sound a battle charge", his love is worth more than all of that.

Planet Waves marked a further progression from the low point of *Self Portrait*. In the Dylan pantheon, it is up there alongside *New Morning* as a revitalised return; but at the time, the album was overshadowed by Dylan's American tour with The Band. It was to be the first full tour since the crazy days of 1966, and eight years away hadn't blunted Dylan's appeal. The 40 dates sold out within minutes; it was the largest-grossing rock 'n' roll tour to date and attracted an unprecedented amount of media attention. After years in the shadows, the tour put Bob Dylan right back under the spotlight.

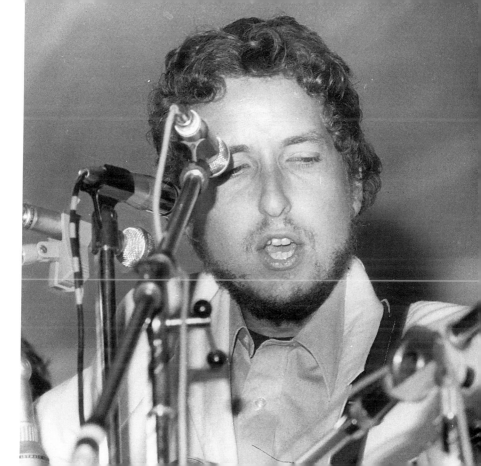

BEFORE THE FLOOD

RELEASED: JUNE 1974. CURRENT ISSUE: CDCBS 22137

Because they were playing such enormous venues (650,000 punters paid $93 million to see 40 shows in 21 days), and because the last time they had been on the road, everyone booed, Bob felt it necessary to shout all the songs. Despite its lack of subtlety though, *Before The Flood* was a necessary souvenir for the 5,350,000 Americans who didn't get tickets, and the millions who weren't even on the same continent.

As Dylan's first official, live album, *Before The Flood* did the business. In the privacy of your own room, you could marvel at his prescience, as he sang about a naked President of the United

States at the same time as Richard Nixon fell from grace, and tumbled out of the White House. After years of obfuscating his past and dodging the punches thrown his way, *Before The Flood* delivered a valuable snapshot of Dylan on the road during 1974.

There was little subtlety or variation in the performances preserved on the double album, everything ('Most Likely You Go Your Way...', 'Lay Lady Lay', 'It Ain't Me Babe') was pitched at the same mid-paced, stadium-filling level. The Band's material was overwhelmed by Garth Hudson's fondness for the clavinette, and came nowhere close to their own epochal double live set *Rock Of Ages* from 1971, while Dylan's acoustic selection ('Don't Think Twice', 'Just Like A Woman', 'It's Alright Ma...') just whetted your appetite for more.

Only in the closing stages did things really start cooking: Dylan borrowed Jimi Hendrix's seething, electric reworking of 'All Along The Watchtower' for his own. He revisited 'Highway 61' and had fun, while 'Like A Rolling Stone' and 'Blowin' In The Wind' bore testament to a talent which, 12 years on, was simply getting stronger and more assured.

The crowds had come to witness the myth made flesh. Any suggestion that Dylan was merely a Sixties' relic were blown away by the avalanche of ticket applications and the subsequent warmth of his reception. With *Planet Waves,* Dylan had indicated that he was able to deal with the Seventies as capably as he had the Sixties; *Before The Flood* marked his willingness to revisit old material. Dylan had been denied the opportunity to be on equal footing with The Beatles in the mid-Sixties; now with The Beatles gone to the four winds, Dylan in 1974 was undeniably rock's biggest attraction. The disillusion he felt about the tour came only in retrospect. At the time, he was glad to be back centre stage.

Written off more times than a stunt pilot, Dylan was buoyant midway through the Seventies. Able at last to come to terms with his legacy, he was also proving that the muse was still an occasional visitor. He was entering the second phase of a career which refused to lie down and die. The Sixties had seen critical praise, the Seventies promised commercial reward. By now, Dylan was one of rock's elder statesmen and all the young punks were at his heels. Having survived the deluge of new Dylans, Bob now had to deal with those who had little time for anyone over 17. The old buzzard still had one shot left in the locker though...

B O B
DYLAN
BLOOD
ON
THE
TRACKS

COMPACT

disc

DIGITAL AUDIO

BLOOD ON THE TRACKS

RELEASED: JANUARY 1975. CURRENT ISSUE: CDCBS 69097

❝I was fighting sentimentality all the way down the line" said Dylan of the album which marked a creative renaissance, and the only album of his which regularly features highly outside his work from the Sixties.

At the time *NME* had Dylan's wife Sara down as "one of rock's least well-known old ladies". Now there was no denying that although publicly Dylan was in a healthy state, privately, his marriage was clearly on edge. Great art rarely springs from contentment; it is produced by turmoil; and as Dylan's 10-year marriage ducked and faltered, the stresses were there for all to see. But the greatness of the songs on *Blood On The Tracks* cannot be ascribed simply to marital discord. Dylan had seen his audience for the first time in eight years and was fired up by his reception on the 1974 tour. Now he was ready to turn the spotlight inwards.

The sessions for *Blood On The Tracks* began in New York in September 1974, but Dylan was dissatisfied with the sound and re-recorded the bulk of the album in Minnesota between Christmas and New Year 1975.

Turmoil never lies far beneath the mask of Dylan's greatness and for him *Blood On The Tracks* was an album of pain. It wasn't all auto-biographical, but it was all from the heart.

Blood On The Tracks is flawed: 'Meet Me In The Morning' is strictly a filler, a bluesy warning of *Street Legal*'s 'New Pony'; 'Lily, Rosemary & The Jack Of Hearts' is convoluted and diverting, but, like a *Forrest Gump* anecdote, you get the uncomfortable feeling that he can't quite remember where (or why) he began it all. 'You're A Big Girl Now' and 'Buckets Of Rain' are minor works masquerading as something far more substantial. At the core of the album are the songs of confession, the dissection of marriage and relationships, the cataclysm.

'Tangled Up In Blue' looks back to Greenwich Village and what has been. Despite Dylan's early covering of his tracks, we can assume that he never worked as a lumberjack or served time on a fishing boat. 'Simple Twist Of Fate' is another of those strong on melancholy, atmospheric songs, recalling 'Visions Of Johanna'. The narrator sits crumpled and huddled in a barren hotel room, reflecting on a mis-spent life, while a solitary saxophone plays out the gloomy soundtrack to his reflections.

'Idiot Wind' is another of those lengthy Dylan songs which aficionados can lose themselves in. With more symbols than a drum kit, 'Idiot Wind' is powered by one of Dylan's most fervent vocals and a smoky, unreal and disquieting sense of atmosphere. There are elements of dislocation, of travel, of Christ crucified and of a Woody Guthrie ramble through the land, tired and torn by Watergate and Vietnam. The 'idiot wind' is blowing from the mouths of senators and congressman, as well as from the other end of disgraced Presidents and their apologists.

'You're Gonna Make Me Lonesome When You Go' is that rarest of things, Bob Dylan trying to be charming. A beguiling, throwaway lilt – Bob rhymes 'Rimbaud' with the title, mentions Ashtabula and sagely reminds us that

"when something's not right, it's wrong".

'Lily, Rosemary & The Jack Of Hearts' has Dylan subverting every Wild West cliché, in much the same way as The Beatles' 'Rocky Raccoon' . All the elements in the song can also be found in John Ford's immortal 1939 movie *Stagecoach* – the gambler, the prostitute with a heart-of-gold, the outlaw, the corrupt businessman. Worth viewing again, if only to hear John Wayne deliver the Dylanesque line: "Seems like a fella can't break out of prison and into society in one week".

'If You See Her, Say Hello' is another unusual card in the Dylan deck, with the narrator down on his knees, snapped by the desertion of his one true love. The song plays on Dylan's unaccustomed vulnerability.

'Shelter From The Storm' is another underrated song, a rich visual tapestry. Doom, Dylan suggests, is all that counts. Toothless men, Ophelia-like flower ladies, a one-eyed undertaker all inhabit a tiny village. A crown of thorns is exchanged, innocence is lost, in a vignette which belongs in a black and white Luis Bunuel film. In fact, a lot of *Blood On The Tracks* has that cinematic feel, perhaps Dylan already had the idea of *Renaldo & Clara* in mind. The strength of *Blood On The Tracks* was that it came in a good three hours under the later film.

With the release of *Blood On The Tracks*, and the adulatory reviews with which it was met worldwide, Dylan was fired and firing. But 1975 was to prove a year of looking back, of shifting the memories of the 1974 tour into smaller, more intimate, unpublicised venues, where, from behind his white-masked face, Dylan could see the whites of his audience's eyes. It was the year of the fresco called The Rolling Thunder Revue. It was also the year which finally, belatedly, saw the release of rock's worst-kept secret.

THE BASEMENT TAPES

RELEASED: AUGUST 1975. CURRENT ISSUE: CBS 4661372

The actual, original 'basement' tape had first been circulated to music publishers in early 1968, pushed around by Dylan's manager, to try and keep interest simmering in an artist who had been glimpsed only at the Woody Guthrie Memorial Concert in January 1968. It was not unlike Colonel Parker trying to keep Elvis in the public eye during his two-year Army service 10 years before. Dylan's people reckoned that his new songs could appeal to diehard fans in the music business, and from that original source tape, Peter, Paul & Mary lifted 'Too Much Of Nothing', The Byrds took 'You Ain't Goin' Nowhere' and 'Nothing Was Delivered', Manfred Mann 'The Mighty Quinn', Julie Driscoll & The Brian Auger Trinity 'This Wheel's On Fire', Fairport Convention 'Million Dollar Bash' and Sandy Denny 'Down In The Flood'.

The songs sprang from sessions between Dylan and The Band in the basement of the group's Woodstock home. The house's name entered rock history with the 1968 release of The Band's début album, *Music From Big Pink*, which included two re-recorded songs, 'Tears Of Rage' and 'I Shall Be Released' from the original Big Pink sessions.

Dylan's demo tape soon began to circulate outside song publishers and went on to form half of rock's first bootleg, *The Great White Wonder* in May 1969. Dylan himself never intended the Woodstock sessions for official release. Too busy pressing on to look back... And so *The Basement Tapes* soon took on the patina of myth, as rumour piled on rumour and fuelled the legend.

Over the years, more and more of the estimated 150 songs recorded by Dylan and The Band at Big Pink, have surfaced on bootleg. If you ever thought that you could never have too much Bob Dylan, an enforced listen to take after take of the bootlegged *Basement Tapes* should dissuade you. That the tapes were never intended for official release is obvious, as Dylan and The Band tinker around

with the slightest of musical jokes – 'See You Later Allen Ginsberg' for example, is just 'See You Later Alligator', but with the poet's name replacing the word 'alligator'. Get the picture?

"I thought everybody had 'em anyway" was Dylan's laid back response when he finally sanctioned the official release of the songs. It was the sound of Bob 'n' the boys letting their hair down, working out on half-remembered rock 'n' roll, folk, blues and country favourites.

The Basement Tapes album featured 24 songs drawn from the daily sessions at Big Pink. The spontaneity of the original 1967 sessions is belied by the subsequent bootlegging of alternate takes and more 'finished' sounding songs. Dylan slipped the not even rumoured 'Goin' To Acapulco' onto the 1975 release, while another unknown basement song, 'Santa Fe' appeared on 1991's *Bootleg Series*.

The Basement Tapes is perhaps rock's most fly-on-the-wall album. Rough and ragged they certainly were, but significantly these songs were flying in the face of the psychedelic and progressive trends of 1967. While The Beatles were trying to find the meaning of life on *Sgt Pepper*, Dylan was singing about buying his girl a herd of moose. While The Rolling

Stones were going '2000 Light Years From Home', Dylan was taking his potatoes down to be mashed!

Songs like 'Odds & Ends', 'Million Dollar Bash', 'Apple Suckling Tree', 'Tiny Montgomery' and 'You Ain't Goin' Nowhere' are rootsy, throwaway, pop songs, just Bob having fun with his buddies. None the worse for that, these songs were his way of easing the pressure. Because they were never intended for public consumption, *The Basement Tapes* are Dylan's way of not being mistaken for America's pre-eminent poet. You could have made a case with songs such as 'Desolation Row' or 'Visions Of Johanna'; you'd be pushed with 'Yea! Heavy And A Bottle Of Bread'.

The songs of real substance: 'Tears Of Rage', 'Too Much Of Nothing', 'Open The Door Homer', 'This Wheel's On Fire', which formed the enduring appeal of *The Basement Tapes*, are as strong as any in the Dylan canon. They speak of timeless truths and half-formed fantasies. 'Tears Of Rage' was an extraordinary accomplishment: written at a time when Jim Morrison was working out his Freudian fantasies on 'The End', 'Tears Of Rage', positively celebrated filial love and despaired of thankless children, as Dylan achingly sang "Oh what kind of love is this, that goes from bad to worse?" 'Too Much Of Nothing' sailed the "waters of oblivion" and Dylan never sounded as wise or messianic as here.

The mythical mist which surrounded *The Basement Tapes* and the eight-year delay in their release, only heightened the mystery. The world was allowed limited access to the basement with the official release sanctioned by Dylan while he was on a roll from *Blood On The Tracks* and his 1974 'comeback' tour. Properly selected, there is still enough unreleased material for a further double CD 'best' of *The Basement Tapes*. It would include the best covers of traditional titles such as 'Bonnie Ship The Diamond', 'Young But Daily Growing', 'Joshua Gone Barbados', 'Wildwood Flower', as well as Hank Williams' 'Stones That You Throw', Brendan Behan's 'The Old Triangle' and Dylan's own spooky 'I'm Not There'.

Finally out of the basement, Bob Dylan set off once again to look for America.

BOB
DYLAN
DESIRE

COMPACT
disc
DIGITAL AUDIO
DIGITALLY MASTERED

DESIRE

RELEASED: JANUARY 1976. CURRENT ISSUE: CDCBS 32570

The Rolling Thunder Revue of Autumn 1975 saw Dylan endeavouring to revive the lost spirit of the freewheeling Sixties. Hitching up with old stalwarts Allen Ginsberg, Joan Baez, Roger McGuinn and Ramblin' Jack Elliott, Dylan also welcomed on board newcomers like T-Bone Burnett, Patti Smith, Ronee Blakely, Scarlet Rivera and David Mansfield.

Rolling Thunder was a direct reaction to the furore of the 1974 tour, as well as a response to the increasing commercialisation and hype of mid-Seventies rock 'n' roll. Rolling Thunder was Greenwich Village on wheels. The studio album that came out of it all reinforced Dylan's social commitment and reflected his personal turmoil.

The opening salvo on *Desire* is the eight-and-a-half minute 'Hurricane', Dylan's plea for the imprisoned boxer Rubin 'Hurricane' Carter. Fitting alongside other Dylan underdogs, Donald White, Medgar Evers and George Jackson, 'Hurricane' rails against wrongful imprisonment, colour prejudice and injustice.

The overall sound of the album is acoustic, Dylan's singing weaving around Rivera's fluid violin and Emmylou Harris' flawless vocals.

The songs drew on Dylan's wild, western memories of New Mexico ('Romance In Durango'); devotional hymns to his wife Sara ('Oh Sister', 'Sara') and another contentious testament to an outlaw, 'Joey'. Joey Gallo was a New York mobster, gunned down by gangsters on the streets of Little Italy. The refrain during this endless exhumation ("what made them want to come and blow you away?") could surely be answered by juggling the words 'reaping' and 'sowing'.

'One More Cup Of Coffee' is another of those great 'lost' Dylan songs, driven by a dark, gypsy atmosphere and fuelled by the menace of a trip to "the valley below". 'Black Diamond Bay' is Joseph Conrad lurking under the volcano. It's Dylan having fun with narrative, juxtaposing who's doing what to whom, then looking down the other end of the telescope after seven incident-packed minutes, and just being at home in that big house by the sea, watching it all on TV anyhow.

Though widely acclaimed as a dense and mysterious Dylan masterpiece, 'Isis' is melodically uninteresting, and seems nailed to the floor by Dylan's rudimentary piano playing. 'Isis' is also a lyrical squib, popping all over the place to no great effect. It is a long and unrewarding journey. Dr Brewer notes that "'to lift the veil of Isis' is to pierce the heart of a great mystery". Dylan fails to take a piece of the heart.

Desire is one of the most frequently forgotten albums in the whole Dylan canon, perhaps because on its release it was overshadowed by the well-reported triumph of Rolling Thunder, or maybe the UK music press was simply too preoccupied by Punk at the time. The album does have its peak moments (the aforementioned 'Joey' and 'Isis', the lightweight 'Mozambique'), but its considerable strengths are too often overlooked.

The whole album has a car boot sale feel to it: Tarot imagery and social conscience; gypsy roamings and Polaroid permanence. *Desire*, in all its flawed perfection, vividly captures the camaraderie of Rolling Thunder and the wayward nature of Dylan's muse.

For the first time on one of his own albums, Dylan collaborated with a co-writer. His partner was the mysterious Jacques Levy, who is acknowledged on seven of the album's nine songs – only the intensely personal 'Oh Sister' and 'Sara' being solo Dylan compositions. Levy had first come to attention through his work with The Byrds' Roger McGuinn, on the ghastly concept of 'Peer Gynt' as rock opera – which gave the world 'Chestnut Mare', that ill-conceived love song to a horse.

Levy pitched into the general turmoil of Rolling Thunder, bolstered the album Dylan needed to reinforce his reputation, and was then gone in the blink of an eye.

There is a beguiling variety and versatility to the music on *Desire,* Emmylou Harris' flawless backing vocals joining in unlikely harmony with Dylan's gravelly delivery. The band Dylan assembled for the album had all cut their teeth on the road, and were already well-versed in dealing with Dylan's sudden switches of direction; but by all accounts, the recording of the album was fraught, even by the standards of Dylan's rollercoaster approach to making records. Musicians had to secondguess the singer and Emmylou spent her time around the microphone having to lip-read to pick up her cues.

The album's closing song, 'Sara' is a more literal devotion than 'Wedding Song' on *Planet Waves*. It is the first song in which Dylan makes reference to an earlier work (writing 'Sad-Eyed Lady Of The Lowlands' in the Chelsea Hotel). At the conclusion to one of his most varied, fragmented and driving albums ever, 'Sara' finishes with the naked plea "Don't ever leave me". In fact, Mrs Dylan walked the following year, and Mr Dylan's private life became very public.

HARD RAIN

RELEASED: SEPTEMBER 1976. CURRENT ISSUE: CDCBS 32308

As the official souvenir of Dylan's most artistically rewarding tour since 1966, *Hard Rain* is tantamount to a lost opportunity. The album was recorded during the second leg of the tour in early 1976, and so missed out on the sprawling, informal intensity of the inaugural shows in late '75, instead substituting rumbustious informality for heartfelt spontaneity.

It is mildly diverting to hear Dylan weaving around the familiar recorded versions of 'One Too Many Mornings' and 'Lay Lady Lay', but as is too often the case with live recordings – and Dylan's in particular – nuance and subtlety are sacrificed to mere volume and swagger.

BOB DYLAN
STREET LEGAL

STREET LEGAL

RELEASED: JUNE 1978. CURRENT ISSUE: CDCBS 86067

Dylan spent 1977 getting divorced and editing the sprawling footage that became the unwatchable, four-hour cinema souvenir of The Rolling Thunder Revue, *Renaldo & Clara*. Faced with an unsettling divorce settlement (rumours had Sara getting $13.5 million), hammered by the critics over his directorial début and encouraged by new manager Jerry Weintraub, Dylan hit the road again in 1978. But this time it was a whole lot different from the guerilla camaraderie of Rolling Thunder.

The tour began in the Far East in early 1978, with Dylan confidently fronting an 11-piece band. The tour was directly at odds with the prevalent punk ethos. It was a bewilderingly showbiz figure who appeared onstage every night for the tour's 114 shows. A courteous, unfailingly polite frontman ("Thank you, that was called 'Maggie's Farm'"). Twelve years on from his last tempestuous appearances in Europe and Australia, the '78 model Dylan returned triumphant. No confrontation this time out as audiences flocked to pay homage to the word-master. With no more Beatles or Elvis, and the prospect of Keith Richards' imprisonment threatening the Stones' future, Dylan was the only *bona-fide* superstar playing the world stage.

The positive critical response to his 1978 tour and the confidence with which Dylan attacked the gruelling schedule, had a lot to do with the fact that he was touring on the back of a strong-sounding new album.

Street Legal was a feast for fans. From its rolling opening moments, 'Changing Of The Guards' sounded like it would be one of the great inscrutable Dylan songs. All the elements were there, and Dylan magisterially handles the final two verses, sounding like Lewis Carroll's White Rabbit on its way to Armageddon "retreating between the King and the Queen of Swords".

Dylan's success was battling with the "enemy within" throughout the album. 'No Time To Think' was a challenging litany of opposites;

'Where Are You Tonight?', a battle for the soul of the singer; while 'Changing Of The Guards' has a "beloved maid... torn between Jupiter and Apollo". With hindsight, the album reveals a Dylan sounding increasingly desperate as he tries to sort out his life. At the time, it sounded like he was brimming over with confidence.

The criticisms which *Street Legal* attracted were as much to do with its sound as its content. At the time, the prevailing Punk propaganda was "anyone can do it"; they weren't going to waste their time in search of the lost chord, any two would do. Ironic, then, that Dylan's most 'produced' album to date, the album he had put most work into, should be released at a time when his original anarchic and unpolished attitudes to recording were being widely adopted by the New Wave.

Much of the appeal of *Street Legal* is derived from its confident opening shot, 'Changing Of The Guards'. The "Sixteen years" which open the song are the period of time between Dylan's fresh-faced début, and the confident-sounding troubador of 1978. The fondness which many fans retain for *Street Legal* has as much to do with its association with those watershed Earl's Court dates, the first opportunity many had to see Bob Dylan since his transformation from folk prophet to Messiah.

'Señor' is driven in tandem by Steve Douglas' sweaty saxophone and Dylan's world-weary lyrics. This is the sound of a man at the end of his tether. Robert Mitchum in some end-of-the-world cantina, down to his last cigarette butt, and a future as bleak as the shadow outside the window.

The album's other outstanding track is the subterranean 'Where Are You Tonight? (Journey Through Dark Heat)'. Percussive and mysterious, the song is haunted by a fragmentary organ, which even draws comparison to the magnificent 'Like A Rolling Stone'.

Maybe it was the rich and abundant texture of the lyrics which suggested yet another Dylan 'comeback', 'No Time To Think' and 'Where Are You Tonight' are as dense and impenetrable as 'Gates Of Eden' more than a decade before. Perhaps it was the confidence with which Dylan sang, and the fullness of the arrangements which bolstered the songs. Whatever the case, *Street Legal* duly delivered.

The lacklustre 'Baby Stop Crying' gave Dylan a Top 20 hit single, placing him alongside The Smurfs, Boney M and Showaddywaddy.

The album was split between the plodding ('New Pony', 'Is Your Love In Vain?') and the magnificent ('Señor', 'Where Are You Tonight?'). 'Señor' is another Tex-Mex border song, suffused with menace. 'True Love Tends To Forget' gives Dylan a chance to rhyme 'forget' with 'Tibet'. 'We Better Talk This Over' is a tortured tale of a stormy relationship. The tormented 'Where Are You Tonight? (Journey Through Dark Heat)' was a bitter and sinuous closing shot. A dense and impenetrable tale of lost dreams, misguided loyalty and misplaced faith; a small glimpse of what was to follow.

BOB DYLAN AT BUDOKAN

RELEASED: MAY 1979. CURRENT ISSUE: DCBS 96004.

Such was the success of the 1978 tour that the pressure was now on to provide the market with a live souvenir. Unfortunately, the double album which emerged was recorded too early in the proceedings to be a worthy reminder of Dylan's most commercially successful and critically acclaimed tour.

Bob Dylan At Budokan at least offers a reminder of just how Dylan had broadened the scope of his source material. Impressed by Bob Marley and the I-Threes' call and response style, Dylan relied heavily on his trio of backing singers. As a result, some of the material ('Mr Tambourine Man', 'Just Like A Woman') does verge perilously close to the Las Vegas style of presentation which critics claimed Dylan was pursuing. But, at its best, Budokan captured the power of the performances: 'Like A Rolling Stone' and 'All Along The Watchtower' were steam-hammered reminders of the impact on audiences. There was a sinewy 'Oh Sister', and reggae-tinged 'Shelter From The Storm' and 'Knockin' On Heaven's Door'. 'Blowin' In The Wind' was starkly and sincerely delivered, while 'The Times They Are A-Changin'' was transformed into a timely and timeless singalong. 'It's Alright Ma (I'm Only Bleeding)' was delivered with a persistent cut and thrust. 'I Want You' moved from bouncing frivolity into dark, brooding introspection.

It was a rewarding journey, and an affecting reminder of many people's first impression of Bob Dylan on a concert stage.

As the 1978 tour wound its way across America, Dylan was soundchecking with an unnamed instrumental piece. When the tour ended, and Dylan found time to unwind, he added words to the melody, and christened it 'Slow Train Coming'.

SLOW TRAIN COMING
BOB DYLAN

SLOW TRAIN COMING

RELEASED: AUGUST 1979. CURRENT ISSUE: CDCBS 32524

If the train was slow, the reaction to Bob Dylan's conversion to "born again" Christianity was swift. From the heights and triumphs of 1978, Dylan in 1979 dipped way down to the valley below, as the critics pounded his first gospel album, and fans stayed away in droves.

This was not a return to the controversies of 1965 or the spirited confrontations of 1966; 1979 saw Dylan as an embittered isolationist, under siege from audiences already smarting from the whiplash of punk, and with the double whammy of Reaganomics and Thatcherism straight ahead.

Dylan may have misjudged the mood of the times. There was certainly a need for spiritual values as the Eighties loomed, but no one wanted the grim Old Testament prophecies proffered by *Slow Train Coming*. The spiritual values Dylan espoused here, were straight-forward, down-the-line, no-nonsense Christianity.

Touring in late 1978, Dylan had found himself in another hotel room: "There was a presence in the room that couldn't have been anybody but Jesus" he said later. The first three months of 1979 were spent in Bible studies: "Jesus put his hand on me. It was a physical thing. I felt my whole body tremble. The glory of the Lord knocked me down and picked me up".

Coming off the back of the triumphant, resurgent 1978 world tour, the news that Jewish rock icon Bob Dylan had become a born-again Christian was too good an opportunity for the media to miss.

Christian imagery had played an important part in Dylan's writing from the very beginning, but the contexts had always been critical and questioning, as in the withering 'With God On Our Side' or tackling the increased commercialisation of religion in 'It's Alright Ma...' By the time of the hymnal 'Forever Young' in 1974, Dylan had God on his side.

In May 1979, Dylan travelled to Muscle Shoals studios in Alabama to record his first 'born-again' album. Mark Knopfler and Pick Withers from Dire Straits were in on the sessions, which were produced by soul veteran Jerry Wexler.

Dylan was keen to bear witness to his conversion, and the best way he knew to evangelise was to make an album. *Slow Train Coming* is not without musical merit; it was the tub-thumping lyrics which fans found hard to take. Ironically, such was Dylan's zeal, that the vocals were handled with a fire and vigour which resulted in Dylan receiving his first ever Grammy award, for 'Best Vocal Performance, Male' on 'Gotta Serve Somebody'.

Gospel music can be rich and rewarding – whatever your feelings about the existence or otherwise of God. Few can help but be moved by Sam Cooke's work with The Soul Stirrers, or the Gospel fervour of The Mighty Clouds Of Joy, the Swan Silvertones or The Jesse Dixon Singers.

Dylan's 'gospel' though, had all the songs pitched in the same one-dimensional key of 'belief'. There was none of the joy of conversion, no desire to sing out and share the rewards of Heaven. Dylan was staring down, into the flames of Hell, and his message was

that it was a long and harrowing journey, through purgatory, to redemption.

The musical disappointment was exacerbated for many longtime fans, who felt betrayed by an album which reeked of rigid rules and fierce intolerance. The man who for so long had personified tolerance and insisted on an open mind, now sang that there was "no neutral ground" when it came to faith or unbelief. There was to be no argument, there were no shades of grey, no longer room for doubt.

'Slow Train' itself was a driving, pounding steam-train of a song, but hearing Dylan sneer at "sheiks walkin' around like kings" made his old-fashioned sermonising seem like the small-town prejudices of a travelling preacher. 'Born-again' songs such as 'Gotta Serve Somebody', 'Gonna Change My Way Of Thinking', 'Do Right To Me Baby (Do Unto Others)' and 'When You Gonna Wake Up?' were written and sung with the zeal of the freshly converted. You can overlook 'Man Gave Names To All The Animals' in the hope that it was written for one of his children, but they must have been a bit old for nursery rhymes by this time.

The songs which endure on *Slow Train*

Coming, are the ebb and flow of 'Precious Angel', 'I Believe In You' (with its debt to the opening lines of 'Smoke Gets In Your Eyes') and the powerful, potent spirituality of 'When He Returns'. It is this last song which, in closing the album, suggests the standard which – given time and objectivity – all the songs on *Slow Train Coming* could have achieved.

But Dylan was impatient to get out and spread the word to the crowds, which meant that in the haste of writing and recording *Slow Train Coming*, the album remains a signpost on a never-ending road.

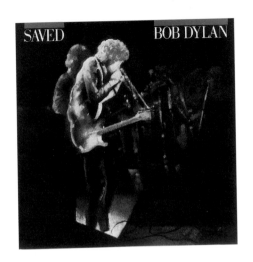

SAVED

RELEASED: JUNE 1980. CURRENT ISSUE: COLCD 32742,

Following the 100-plus sold-out shows at spectacular venues around the world during 1978, Dylan's first live performances of 1979 came during a 14-night residency at San Francisco's compact Fox-Warfield Theater. Determined to stand firm, Dylan's shows were all defiantly drawn from his 'born-again' work – he played nothing from before *Slow Train Coming*. Fans expecting a 'Greatest Hits' package similar to '78 were loudly and bitterly disappointed.

Dylan refused to bow to public pressure and persevered with his 'inspirational' music. But Dylan seemed to be the only one drawing inspiration, fans and critics were increasingly disappointed and dejected by his tunnel-vision. He was now delivering homophobic rants from the concert stage, while on record remaining as entrenched as ever.

Looking back on the man he had discovered and championed throughout his creative life, Robert Shelton wrote of this period: "Dylan was swimming against the tide, and, I fear, mistaking his role of misunderstood combatant for past similar roles in which he was simply running too far ahead of the consciousness of his audiences".

Shelton was not alone in being disillusioned by Dylan's new music, *Saved* stands as one of Dylan's lowest-selling albums ever. While Christian audiences recognised the coup of having Dylan on their side, the record-buying bulk of his audience rejected his second album of intense, devotional music. Even from the outside sleeve, the album simply looked shoddy, while inside Dylan seemed almost wilfully out of step with the times.

Opening with the old Porter Wagoner Country standard, 'A Satisfied Mind', *Saved* moved doggedly along the same tracks as *Slow Train Coming*. The title song was fiery and straight out of the hellfire preaching and salvation tradition of Elmer Gantry. 'Solid Rock', 'Pressing On' and 'Are You Ready?' were all cut from the same cloth.

'In The Garden' and 'Saving Grace' were less hammering, but Dylan remained intransigent. Salvation, achievable only through the renunciation of sin, was the only answer. He looked around him and saw an immoral world, a world devoid of spiritual values, with Armageddon waiting just around the corner. Apocalypse was high on the menu. It was not a comfortable vision.

Dylan recognised that people were having problems with his transition: "It would have been easier if I'd become a junkie, or a Buddhist, or a Scientologist". But it was not only the intensity of his conversion or the single-mindedness of his vision which many found intimidating; there was also the disturbing association of 'born-again' Christianity with the most extreme Right Wing values, in an America labouring under its first term of the Reagan Presidency.

What Bob Dylan did during 1979 and 1980, he did for himself. He always had done, but this time his slow train just wasn't picking up as many passengers as his odysseys down Highway 61. By the end of 1980, however, Dylan was set to make a detour.

SHOT OF LOVE

RELEASED: AUGUST 1981. CURRENT ISSUE: COL4678392

With his 1980 concerts at the Fox-Warfield Theater, Dylan tempered the religious material with time-honoured favourites. *Shot Of Love* was the final part of Dylan's 'born-again' trilogy, and marked the beginning of a reconciliation between his art and his belief. This was Dylan's most secular album in three years, and the first 'inspirational' album which seemed genuinely to be inspired by a creative, rather than a spiritual impetus.

The title track was produced by Robert 'Bumps' Blackwell, who had worked on the original Little Richard hits which had so thrilled the teenage Bob Zimmerman: "I gotta say that of all the producers I ever used, he had the best instincts, but *Shot Of Love* didn't fit into the current formula. It probably never will. Anyway, people were always looking for some excuse to write me off, and this was as good as any".

The reviews were the most encouraging of the decade so far, although critics worried that Dylan was simply tempering his poor-selling Christian records with calculated non-religious material. But even the devotional 'Shot Of Love', 'Property Of Jesus', 'Dead Man, Dead Man' and 'Trouble' were among the best of Dylan's Gospel work.

'Heart Of Mine' was a beguiling ballad, which – had it appeared in any other context –would have been hailed as a highlight. 'Lenny Bruce' was predictably seized upon, as it had Dylan looking back to the halcyon days of Greenwich Village café society. In the song Dylan somehow managed to make his memories of the innovative comedian, who died from a drugs overdose in 1966, seem both trite ("I rode with him in a taxi once... seemed like it took a couple of months") and touchingly sincere ("he was the brother you never had").

Although recorded at the *Shot Of Love* sessions, 'The Groom's Still Waiting At The Altar' was only released as the B-side of 'Heart Of Mine' – an America-only single – during 1981. The CD release finds it restored to its proper context; a pounding, scathing world-view, it is reminiscent of the panorama seen from 'Desolation Row' half a lifetime before.

Shot Of Love also boasted two songs which confirmed that, however wonky his spiritual vision may have been, Dylan could still focus his songwriting genius. 'In The Summertime' has Bob's weariest vocal, at odds with the uplifting theme of the song. If only all Dylan's inspirational songs had been of this high calibre, he might not have fought such a lonely battle.

'Every Grain Of Sand', bewilderingly written for Euro MP Nana Mouskouri, concluded the album. Basking beneath God's beneficence, Bob sings of seeing the Maker's hand in every living thing. Drawing heavily on William Blake's 'Auguries Of Innocence', 'Every Grain Of Sand' also recalls Dylan's own early sense of wonder, as found on 'Mr Tambourine Man' and 'Lay Down Your Weary Tune'. It was a stately, refined conclusion for the latest in a line of albums which had seemed to hold out the promise of a Dylan 'comeback'.

With Shot Of Love to promote, Dylan undertook a truncated European tour during July 1981, leavening his spiritual music with a sprinkling of secular favourites. The notices were politely receptive, but still a long way removed from the ecstatic notices of 1978.

It was to be a long and dusty road through the Eighties, and Bob Dylan still had a long way to travel.

BOB DYLAN

INFIDELS

INFIDELS

RELEASED: NOVEMBER 1983. CURRENT ISSUE: CBS4607272

Infidels threatened to do for Bob Dylan in the Eighties, what *Blood On The Tracks* had achieved in the Seventies – a total, triumphant rebirth. Written off frequently since 1963, but still defiantly surviving every musical sea-change, Dylan was overdue a new audience: an audience who had grown up since punk, and paid allegiance not to LP records and the music press, but Compact Discs and MTV.

There was a feeling that the time was right. Longtime Dylan-fan Mark Knopfler was asked in to oversee the album production; in the four years since he had guested on *Slow Train Coming*, Dire Straits had gone on to become one of the rock world's biggest attractions. Dylan also roped in the ubiquitous rhythm section of Sly & Robbie, while ex-Rolling Stone Mick Taylor was showcased as lead guitarist.

Infidels was intended to bring Dylan to the attention of that massive new MTV audience. The Biblical imagery was back-projected here, not centre-stage. The original, Knopfler-produced *Infidels* could well have gained Dylan a foothold with that audience, fond of the rootsy new American music of REM, Jason & The Scorchers and Los Lobos. But Dylan tilted the album off-kilter by ditching the magnificent 'Blind Willie McTell', the driving 'Foot Of Pride' and the pounding 'Julius & Ethel'. What we got instead was the parochial 'Union Sundown', a song hard to reconcile with the man who had written 'North Country Blues' 20 years before.

'Blind Willie McTell' became the Holy Grail for Dylan collectors during the 1980s, like 'Farewell Angelina' from 1965, the song quickly took on mythic proportion, but actually lived up to expectation when it was finally released on *The Bootleg Series* in 1991.

What was left on *Infidels* was the usual Dylan/Gemini battle between good and bad. 'Jokerman', 'Sweetheart Like You' and 'License To Kill' sit happily among Dylan's best work of the decade. 'Man Of Peace', while undeniably cautionary about the danger of Satan, had enough Dylan twists and turns to rise above the plodding, devotional material from *Saved*. 'Neighbourhood Bully' could have been about Israel, which seemed a further distancing from Dylan's 'born-again' beliefs. 'I And I' owed a heavy debt to Bob Marley's Rastafarian beliefs, while 'Don't Fall Apart On Me Tonight' provided a triumphant, pleading conclusion. Dylan had rarely sounded as vulnerable as he did here.

Flawed, but just about passing muster – Mark Knopfler wasn't the only one unhappy with the finished *Infidels*. The feeling was that, given the Knopfler production, had Dylan toed the line and stuck with the original choice of material, *Infidels* could have been the masterpiece he needed to win himself a big new Eighties audience, rather than having to rely on the Sixties survivors who still slavishly followed his every move.

But this was proving to be par for the course for Dylan during the 1980s. Following his 'born-again' conversion, on record, he had been uncertain and cautionary. The very best had Dylan still capable of matching the right words, in just the right order, to achieve maximum impact, his voice keening and poignant. Balance that against the very worst: diatribes rasped out against leaden backing tracks, passion reduced to knee-jerk response. Guess which Bob favoured releasing?

Indeed, one of the few constants throughout Dylan's career has been his total lack of quality control. Few would deny the quality of his writing (his singing may still leave some cold, but even people who hate Bob Dylan can appreciate the influence of Bob Dylan's words). What Dylan manifestly never had, was any appreciation of his own abilities. He has always maintained that he could make *Blonde On Blonde* again tomorrow, but no one would appreciate it. In his mind, *Infidels* stacks up against *Freewheelin'*. Dylan believes as much in his new material as we treasure his old.

Dylan definitely and defiantly refuses to be weighed down by the past. That is to his credit; he is also the only major figure from the Sixties who has consistently refused tour sponsorship, and was one of the last to lease his songs for commercial use. He simply will not play the corporate rock star game.

Dylan's strength has always been his music, but he seems to be the last person to appreciate that. To leave the stunning 'Blind Willie McTell' off *Infidels*, and replace it with the plodding 'Union Sundown' suggests either sheer contrariness or a critical faculty way out of whack. But then, Bob wrote both songs, and I guess it's ultimately up to him which he prefers.

Bob Dylan
Real Live

REAL LIVE

RELEASED: DECEMBER 1984. CURRENT ISSUE: COL4678412

Promoter Bill Graham had urged Dylan back on the road during 1984, with another of Graham's clients, Carlos Santana, as 'Special Guest'. Dylan's attitude to live work was revealing. Beginning life as an acoustic performer, he held audiences solo and spellbound, until playing onstage alone no longer appealed to him. Working with an electric band during the head-on collision which was the 1966 world tour, soured Dylan's attitude to live work, but the equipment, PA and amplification was antediluvian back then. The 1974 tour was tightly disciplined, but, in retrospect, an empty experience. Then there was the ramshackle carnival atmosphere, spread over four hours most nights, with past and present mingling on The Rolling Thunder Revue.

During 1978, the response was ecstatic. Demand for the first post-Born-Again tour of 1981 and his 1984 European jaunt saw Dylan playing in large venues, to fans baying for the old familiar songs. Dylan usually went out of his way to supply those old familiar songs, he just had a tendency to, at best, mangle them, or at worst, render them unrecognisable.

The 1984 touring band commemorated on *Real Live* featured Brit-Rock veterans Mick Taylor and Ian McLagen (from The Faces). Predictably perverse, Dylan had picked up an LA punk band The Cruzados to back him on a prestigious TV slot with David Letterman in March 1984. They had run through dozens of songs, but just as they took to the air for the live broadcast, Dylan started playing Sonny Boy Williamson's 'Don't Start Me Talking', one of the few songs they had never even talked about, let alone rehearsed. As it happened, the Letterman show was the fillip Bob needed, and The Cruzados would have made a perfect band to back Dylan on tour. They didn't, which goes some way to explaining the lacklustre, stadium-oriented *Real Live*.

The crowd-pleasing solo 'It Ain't Me Babe' and 'Girl From The North Country' reveal the inherent weakness of Dylan trying to pitch his reedy voice way back to the bleachers. 'I And I' and 'License To Kill' marked little real improvement on their studio début barely a year before. Too many opportunities were seized by Mick Taylor for extended guitar solos, while the rhythm section of Greg Sutton and Colin Allen were left blindly following Bob's baffling lead.

'Maggie's Farm', 'Ballad Of A Thin Man' and 'Masters Of War' were fist-in-the-air crowd-pleasers, all right on the night. The rarely performed 'Tombstone Blues' was given a welcome airing, with Santana's rollicking guitar fully in keeping with the song's levity.

That aside, the album is worth owning for the seven-minute, solo 'Tangled Up In Blue', a version Dylan admitted he preferred to the original version from *Blood On The Tracks*. Shifting perspective, time and place, Dylan sounds eerily at ease with this disjointed and haunting version.

The final date on Dylan's 1984 tour was at Slane Castle, near Dublin. 'Special Guests' had been the order of the day during those summer dates. As well as the old guard of Joan Baez, Eric Clapton and Van Morrison, young pretenders like Chrissie Hynde and U2's Bono had, at various points during the tour, clambered onstage to join the venerable, and venerated, Bob.

The tour at least suggested that, unlike his contemporaries coasting on the past, Dylan – busy reconciling what had been with what was to come – was set to reclaim the future.

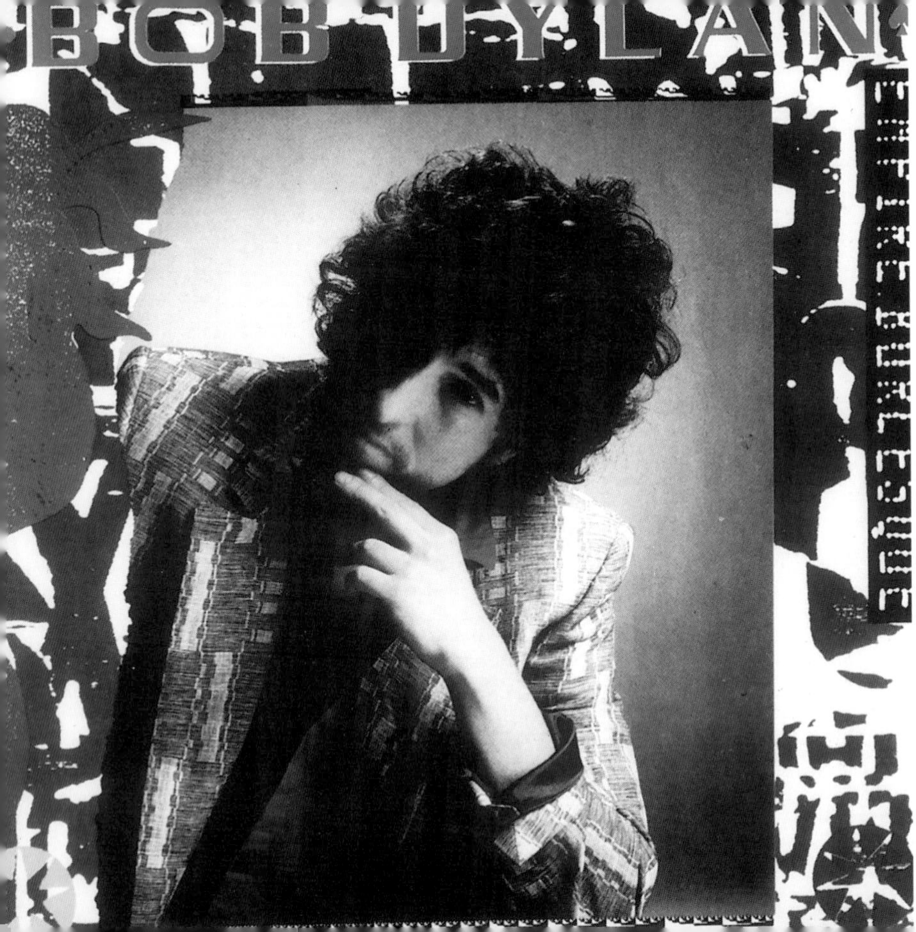
BOB DYLAN

EMPIRE BURLESQUE

RELEASED: JUNE 1985. CURRENT ISSUE: COL4678402.

T he sessions leading up to *Empire Burlesque* were fraught. Dylan had been plainly uncomfortable with the new technology now inherent in the recording industry. He was always one for going in and bashing it down with as few frills and as little fuss as possible – his fourth album had been recorded in one evening; the bulk of the acoustic side of *Bringing It All Back Home* in one action-packed afternoon. Now, confronted with the necessity of making himself sound '80s', Dylan was reluctantly coerced into dealing with the modern world.

Dylan had reluctantly joined the video age with promos for 'Sweetheart Like You' and 'Jokerman' from *Infidels,* but neither had set the pulses of the MTV couch-potatoes racing. Although his eye was set over his shoulder (planning the release of the retrospective box-set *Biograph* and approving the publication of *Lyrics, 1962 - 1985*, an updated edition of 1973's *Writings & Drawings*), Dylan knew that 1985 had to see a brand *new* album.

Empire Burlesque is as good an indication as any of where Bob Dylan was at during the mid-Eighties. This is the great utility Bob Dylan album, there is stately, solo acoustic ('Dark Eyes'), frenetic gospel style call and response ('Tight Connection To My Heart'), couldn't

give a shit rock 'n' roll ('Clean Cut Kid'), dreary fillers ('Trust Yourself', 'Never Gonna Be The Same Again', 'Something's Burning Baby'), a love song addressed to Elizabeth Taylor ('Emotionally Yours') and one huge, epic, searing moment ('When The Night Comes Falling From The Sky').

Fans wanted this to be the triumphant Dylan return. On the bootleg network, people knew of the existence of searing new songs such as 'Blind Willie McTell', 'Foot Of Pride', 'Angelina' and 'Tell Me'. Recorded at five studios over a period of months, *Empire Burlesque* would surely be the reward for such dedicated following?

Well, up to a point. In terms of number of

songs recorded, the period 1982/83 was Dylan's most productive in 20 years, but the released results were patchy. What could have been triumphant too often ended up settling for adequate. Only in hindsight did Dylan come to realise that his strength lay in being Bob Dylan, not trying to be Michael Bolton.

Early in 1985, Dylan recorded a version of 'When The Night Comes Falling From The Sky' with two members of Bruce Springsteen's E. Street Band, guitarist Steve Van Zandt and pianist Roy Bittan. Springsteen was the only one of the Seventies 'new Dylans' to come within snapping distance of the old, and the drive provided by his musicians (the version was made available on *The Bootleg Series*) was revealing, you can hear Dylan's enthusiasm brim over as the band crank up another gear, and pound the song home.

The version which appeared on *Empire Burlesque* had been handled by remix maestro Arthur Baker, and was Dylan's biggest-sounding song ever, although long-time fans wondered why Bob Dylan wanted to sound like New Order.

Empire Burlesque sits half-way through the

decade that Bob Dylan had such problems coping with. All down the years, he has worked on instinct and his own judgement. His first and most influential manager Albert Grossman established him, and since the cessation of their troubled relationship in 1967, Dylan has missed the firm guiding hand of a Grossman – even as their relationship trailed through the law courts in the 1980s.

Even if he had a manager who was wholly clued in to the direction Dylan should take, there is no guarantee he would have challenged his client ("So I'll replace 'Blind Willie McTell' with 'Union Sundown' then?" "Sounds good to me Bob, you're not paying me a six figure salary to disagree with you").

Empire Burlesque at least displayed Dylan beginning to understand what he was good at and what was wanted of him, as his professional career approached the 25-year mark.

With the rumoured release of the long-over-due box set as well as his most polished album of the decade, Dylan fans were finally getting the return they felt they were owed, in what had proven to be Dylan's patchiest professional decade to date. Things, the word went, were looking up.

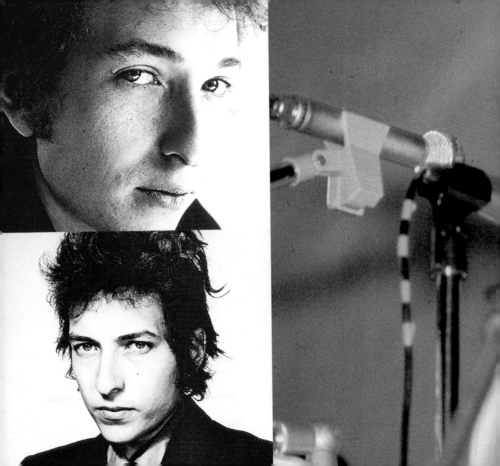

Then came Live Aid.

In typical Dylan style, when he made a klutz of himself, he chose to do it in front of the largest television audience ever. Accompanied by Rolling Stones Ron Wood and Keith Richards (who was going through one of his not-talking-to-Mick phases) Dylan dispatched his career down the dumper.

Introduced by Jack Nicholson as one of "America's great voices of freedom", Dylan looked and sounded like he'd swallowed his harmonica. His performance on July 13, 1985 confirmed what every Dylan-hater knew all along anyhow: he couldn't sing for toffee and his harmonica playing was about as good as Stevie Wonder's table tennis.

You couldn't quibble with Dylan's choice of material though; the line about "the whole wide world is watching" leapt right out of 'When The Ship Comes In'. And there were reasons for the embarrassment – because of running times, there hadn't been time for a sound-check, the onstage monitors were switched off, and while Dylan couldn't hear himself sing, what he could hear was the all-star ensemble rehearsing 'We Are The World' just a few feet away behind the onstage curtain.

Dylan's mumbled pronouncement about the desperate plight of the American farmers even became the inspiration for that year's Farm Aid. In which case, at least something was salvaged out of Dylan's disastrous Live Aid performance, which Bob Geldof later admitted was, for him, the low point of the whole event.

Asked by Willie Nelson to help inaugurate Farm Aid in September 1985, Dylan was determined not to take another televised pratfall. Tom Petty received a telephone call out of the blue, and thus began a fruitful live association between Dylan and Petty's band, The Heartbreakers. Unfortunately, that hand in glove partnership was never fully realised on record.

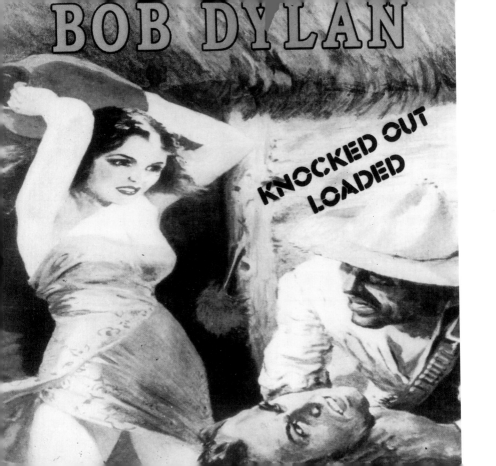

KNOCKED OUT LOADED

RELEASED: JULY 1986. CURRENT ISSUE: CBS 4670402

Hidebound by the experience of working with the new technology, Dylan was keen to shuck that studio discipline in favour of his usual spontaneous way of working. He rounded up Tom Petty & The Heartbreakers and settled into a recording studio, determined to cut his new album in under a week. Just like the old days. Except that, in the old days, Dylan had plenty to say, and could say it alone. Reports of the sessions with Petty's band in March 1986 were, predictably, encouraging. Equally predictably, what ended up on the finished record was a pale shadow of what might have been.

The outstanding track from *Knocked Out Loaded* was the 11-minute collaboration with playwright Sam Shepard. Shepard had been a drummer with The Holy Modal Rounders, partner to punk poet Patti Smith and had won the Pulitzer prize in 1979, four years after he had served as the official diarist on the Rolling Thunder Revue. By the time he collaborated with Dylan again on *Knocked Out Loaded*, Shepard was breaking hearts as a heart-throb movie star.

'Brownsville Girl' had begun life as 'New Danville Girl' in late 1984. Two years later, the rewritten song was the highlight of another in a long series of weak Dylan albums. The song rambles and sprawls, but contains some of that essential mystery necessary for Dylan's best work. Sparked off by viewing a Gregory Peck film, *The Gunfighter*, 'Brownsville Girl' recounts the problems posed by the burden of fame and responsibility. The film dealt with the public image of a legendary man, and with the disciples waiting none too patiently in the wings. Peck's character was tired of the attention lavished on him and was keen to settle down quietly to get on with his own life. You can see what would appeal to Bob Dylan in a film like that.

Al Kooper, a Dylan collaborator from the mid-Sixties, was involved in some of the early *Knocked Out Loaded* sessions, and he revealed that on the original, "there was more stuff" equally as exciting as 'Brownsville Girl'. Indeed, *Rolling Stone* writer Mikal Gilmore, who had been privy to the original Dylan and Petty rehearsals for the album, wrote a glowing piece which claimed that Los Lobos were scheduled for the album as well, and that Dylan and his new backing band had at least 20 "Chicago-steeped blues" as well as R&B, gospel and hillbilly rock, all intended for what ultimately became the limp *Knocked Out Loaded*.

The album opened with a cover of Junior Parker's 'You Wanna Ramble' but the version lacked fire. The old Country standard, 'Precious Memories' – a favourite of Roy Acuff, Jim Reeves and Willie Nelson – was unhappily set to a half-hearted reggae rhythm. Too frequently, Dylan relied on a wailing chorus of female backing vocalists. It had worked well in 1978. But by 1986 it was palling, and only emphasised the inherent weakness of the material.

'Brownsville Girl' sat uneasily among lacklustre Dylan originals such as 'Maybe Someday' or 'Driftin' Too Far From Shore'.

Even a collaboration with Brill Building graduate Carole Bayer Sager ('Under Your Spell'), barely matched her Sixties pop sensibility. It was all part of the album's failure, of a grand idea going off at half-cock.

You can salute Dylan's desire to bypass the increasing reliance on studio wizardry, and just get on with making records. He had done it 10 years before on *Desire*, but that album had been sustained by some of his best ever songs. *Knocked Out Loaded* groaned under weak and insubstantial songs, like the ersatz gospel of Kris Kristofferson's 'They Killed Him', which compounded its ghastliness by having the chorus sung by a children's choir!

Knocked Out Loaded lacked anything approaching the spark and flair one used to associate with Bob Dylan, still widely perceived as pop's pre-eminent composer.

Ah well, reasoned fans, the one consolation after Live Aid and *Knocked Out Loaded*, was that at least things couldn't get any worse.

Then Bob decided he wanted to be an actor...

HEARTS OF FIRE

RELEASED: SEPTEMBER 1987. CURRENT ISSUE: CBS 40870

❝At one time, Billy Parker (Bob Dylan) was the biggest name in rock, a legend, whose music was an inspiration to millions. But when the pressure of fame became too much, he turned his back on it all"... "Oh God", groaned everyone who read the official synopsis of *Hearts Of Fire*, which opened in London in October 1987. It ran for a matter of weeks, then disappeared into video limbo.

Hearts Of Fire had sounded bad enough at the press conference, held at the National Film Theatre on London's South Bank the previous August. Director Richard Marquand, who was to die of a heart attack barely weeks before the film's opening, was obviously ecstatic at having snared Bob Dylan for the role of the legendary Billy Parker. Dylan himself looked like he was already beginning to have second thoughts.

After reading through the synopsis, and hearing Marquand enthusing about his re-interpretation of the old Hollywood chestnut *A Star Is Born*, it was critic Philip Norman who voiced the thoughts of most of the hacks present, when he asked Dylan something along the lines of: "Why are you wasting your time with this crap?"

Prior to filming, Dylan undertook a lengthy tour of Australasia and North America with Tom Petty & The Heartbreakers. The rest of 1986 was taken up with filming *Hearts Of Fire*. The soundtrack album must have taken at least one afternoon.

The initial curiosity, of hearing how Rupert Everett handled Soft Cell's 'Tainted Love', or whether Fiona Flanagan's version of 'Let The Good Times Roll' was a cover of the Shirley & Lee classic, soon passed. Fiona's immediate family aside, Bob Dylan was the reason people purchased the soundtrack album. Dylan was clearly struggling, contributing only two original songs to the soundtrack album – one of which, 'Had A Dream About You, Baby' – obviously impressed

the composer so much, that he also included it on his next studio album, *Down In The Groove*.

As well as Dylan's own lacklustre 'Night After Night', *Hearts Of Fire* also featured his cover of John Hiatt's 'The Usual', although inexplicably, Dylan's best musical moment from the film was excluded – a cover of Dr Hook's 'Couple More Years', touchingly performed solo and acoustic in a barn to entice Fiona. It received a hearty drubbing, and even Dylan looked like he would struggle to recover his momentum. But despite all his very public and very obvious failings during the 1980s, Dylan was still held in high esteem by his peers and disciples. He joined U2 on their mega-platinum *Rattle & Hum* set of 1988, was prominently featured on USA For Africa's 'We Are The World' and Artists Against Apartheid's 'Sun City'.

The combination of Bob Dylan and Tom Petty & The Heartbreakers was still proving a potent draw on the live concert circuit, but that in-concert dynamism had yet to be translated onto vinyl, as we still thought of it back then. Dylan was a notoriously erratic live performer, and following his disappointing experiments with video and film, what was needed was a dynamite album to prove he could still pack a punch. He wasn't about to deliver that, at least, not yet.

BOB DYLAN

Down In The Groove

DOWN IN THE GROOVE

RELEASED: JUNE 1988. CURRENT ISSUE: CBS 4602672

The irony was that Bob Dylan, of all people, was experiencing writer's block. For 20 years, songs had poured out of Dylan in a torrent. Some good, some bad, some magnificent, many unreleased. There were whole albums' worth of songs which Dylan had never sanctioned for official release, but which had made their way onto the thriving and insatiable bootleg market.

Still on the ropes following the reviews of *Hearts Of Fire*, Dylan's muse was on permanent hold. Collaborations with Tom Petty, Carole Bayer Sager, The Grateful Dead; covers of John Hiatt, old blues and gospel songs, all were clear indicators that Dylan was struggling with his own muse.

During 1987, Dylan considered making a whole album of cover versions. Comparisons were made with 1970's iconoclastic *Self Portrait*. There were those who felt that much of Dylan's 1980's work comprised loose variations on *Self Portrait*. After that bomb, he had struck back with *New Morning*, *Planet Waves* and *Blood On The Tracks*. But the 1980s were drawing to a close, and Dylan was already two strikes down.

In interviews, Dylan was talking of recording songs popularised by Frank Sinatra, Peggy Lee and Bing Crosby. Dylan was still a few years ahead of the likes of Sinéad O'Connor, Shawn Colvin, Michael Bolton and Annie Lennox, who in the Nineties have recorded whole albums of cover versions.

Of course, during a professional career which was marching up to its quarter century, Dylan had included innumerable cover versions both in concert and on record – by his own admission, at the beginning of his career, he was little more than a "Woody Guthrie jukebox". But Bob Dylan, the man who had dragged pop music kicking and screaming into the 1960s; Bob Dylan, rock's first poet; Bob Dylan, the man who had given rock 'n' roll a conscience, pop a sense of social responsibility... Bob Dylan recording an album of songs by Bing Crosby?

The incredulity overlooked Dylan's age. Born in 1941, Dylan's own pre-rock 'n' roll idols included both the hip (Hank Williams, Woody Guthrie, John Lee Hooker) and the tragically un-hip (Johnnie Ray, Dinah Shore). The advent of rock 'n' roll in the mid-Fifties hit the young Bob Zimmerman with the same thunderbolt impact as hundreds of thousands of disaffected teenagers around the world.

On Presley's death, Dylan recalled that "hearing Elvis for the first time was like busting out of jail". Bob Zimmerman's first known original song was 1958's 'Hey Little Richard'. The seeds were there for an entire album of covers, but by 1988, it indicated a serious case of writer's block from the writer by whom others were measured. In the event Dylan did manage to muster four original tracks for the new album, two of them joint compositions with Robert Hunter – lyricist of The Grateful Dead.

On its release, *Down In The Groove* was harshly condemned, perhaps looking back, a little too harshly. Listening to it again, I was struck by the eerie, beautiful air of melancholy which Dylan injects into three songs – 'Death Is Not The End', 'Ninety Miles An Hour (Down A Dead End Street)' and 'Rank Strangers To Me'. Dylan had never sounded more funereal, never more wistful and reflective, never more aware of his own mortality than here.

With the songs of his 'born-again' conversion still ringing in our ears, Dylan's bleak and austere trilogy here suggested little in the way of salvation or redemption. The very title, 'Death Is Not The End', did not offer any hope. The death Dylan anticipated here was not one in which he would pass through the pearly gates and enter into Paradise. This death was simply a prolonging of the suffering and agonies of life.

Hank Snow's 'Ninety Miles An Hour (Down A Dead End Street)' was also a death song imbued with a true morbidity, while on the album's closing track 'Rank Strangers To Me', Dylan had never sounded bleaker nor more stripped of hope. All the people the singer encounters at his childhood home are 'rank strangers'. The eerie atmosphere of the song, the sense of futility, is highlighted by Larry Klein's spectral bass notes. Maybe, Dylan suggests, death will offer some salvation, although judging from the singer's tone in this song, it isn't worth holding your breath for.

Those three songs, plus a spirited rendition of the old folk favourite 'Shenandoah', gave an indication of just how powerful *Down In The Groove* could have been. But by then, most people had given up making excuses for Bob Dylan.

Proof was now desperately needed that Dylan was still a player. *Down In The Groove* wasn't the necessary evidence. Kicking off with an unremarkable cover of Wilbur Harrison's 'Let's Stick Together' (previously hammered to death by Canned Heat and Bryan Ferry), *Down In The Groove*'s sparse 32 minutes screamed that Bob Dylan had lost it.

At a time when compact discs were literally stretching pop's boundaries – cramming up to 75 minutes of music onto a shiny CD as opposed to vinyl's parsimonious 40 – *Down In The Groove*, with only a sprinkling of Dylan originals spread thin over a whole album, looked and sounded like an epitaph. But, as the man said, 'Death Is Not The End'.

DYLAN & THE DEAD

RELEASED: FEBRUARY 1989. CURRENT ISSUE: CBS 4633812

T he loyalty of Dylan's fans was eclipsed only by that of the devoted Deadheads. The Grateful Dead fan army followed the band around the States, pitching their banners, like a cohort of Roman legionaries.

Neither faction was enchanted by *Dylan & The Dead*, an album culled from the half a dozen stadium shows performed by Dylan and the venerable hippie band during the summer of 1987. Rumour had Dylan forgetting all about the recordings, until the tapes were dusted down two years later, and then giving a perfunctory nod to their release.

Historically, the main interest of *Dylan & The Dead* is that it marked the first live version of 'Queen Jane Approximately'. It also marked the nadir of Dylan's recording career. Bob Dylan and The Grateful Dead wading through the unlistenable 'Joey' is an all-time low. The lukewarm versions of 'Slow Train' and 'Gotta Serve Somebody' do little justice to either party, while the singalong finale of 'Knockin' On Heaven's Door' sounds like it was recorded while all concerned were on Mogadon rather than any of the Dead's preferred, consciousness-enhancing chemicals.

It was a marriage made in hell, and the last word should go to the Dead's drummer, Mickey Hart: "We were trying to back up a singer on songs that no one knew. It was not our finest hour, nor his. I don't know why it was even made into a record."

But things were, finally, belatedly, looking up. George Harrison initially only wanted to borrow some home studio time, but ended up taking Dylan on board as a Traveling Wilbury during 1988. Ironically, it was his enrolment as a Wilbury which gave Dylan his biggest commercial success of the decade.

The camaraderie of fictional supergroup The Traveling Wilburys allowed Dylan, Harrison, Tom Petty, Jeff Lynne and the late great Roy Orbison to leave the pressures of their individual stardom behind and regain a degree of anonymity. As a result, the music which appeared on the band's two albums in 1988 and 1990 is among the stars' most engaging and spontaneous.

Perhaps it was the breathing space bought for him by the Wilburys which helped Dylan tap back into his own writing. Certainly his creativity seemed liberated as the 1980s dimmed, and Dylan – with a timely flourish – produced his finest album of the decade.

OH MERCY

RELEASED: OCTOBER 1989. CURRENT ISSUE: CBS 4658002

Tantalisingly, as was so often the way with vintage Dylan albums, *Oh Mercy* could have been even better than it was. The inclusion of 'Series Of Dreams' and 'Dignity', in place of 'Most Of The Time' and 'What Was It You Wanted?', would have transformed the merely magnificent into the epic. As it was, most fans settled gratefully for a return to form, so overdue that it had seemed increasingly like a forlorn hope. Much of the credit was attributed to producer Daniel Lanois, who had worked wonders with U2, Peter Gabriel and Robbie Robertson before sprinkling some fairy dust on his most illustrious client.

The success of *Oh Mercy* certainly owed much to Lanois' sympathetic and atmospheric production, and something to the late night, smoky atmosphere of New Orleans – where the album was recorded in a turn of the century bordello – which inveigled its way onto the finished album. But the chief reason was Dylan's conquering of the writer's block which had dogged his last two albums.

In an interview around the time of the album's release, Dylan admitted he had tackled the problem head-on: "It was either come up with a bunch of songs that were original and pay attention to them, or get some other real good songwriters to write me some songs... Everybody works in the shadow of what they've previously done, but you have to overcome that."

Dylan overcame it magnificently. On the album's standout track, 'Man In The Long Black Coat', Dylan had never sounded more menacing, like he was one of the gangsters freed from Sergio Leone's *Once Upon A Time In The West*, stalking the leaf-strewn streets, as the hurricane breeze bent the New Orleans' trees. The song's air of menace was enhanced by the background atmospherics. 'Man In The Long Black Coat' is all the more remarkable when you consider that it was written in the studio, and put down in one take.

Oh Mercy had Dylan sounding better than ever on a selection of some of his best songs of the decade. There was, of course, some dead wood in the package – 'Most Of The Time' meandered while 'What Was It You Wanted?' sounded more important than what it actually said and 'Political World' read like a knee-jerk song of the moment.

But when he was good, he was very, very good: 'Where Teardrops Fall' was maudlin and heart-tuggingly simple, with Dylan sounding as sincere as one of his vintage C&W heroes; you could just imagine Roy Acuff or Porter Wagoner relishing a song like this.

'Everything Is Broken' was Dylan's current world view. He had failed to find lasting salvation in faith, and everywhere he looked – in politics, in relationships – everything was shattering. If, at times, it tips toward being a shopping list of a song, Dylan's dignified reading saves the day.

'Ring Them Bells' was as opaque and mysterious as any long-time fan could wish for. Visions of the apocalypse, church bells ringing, sacred cows, lost sheep... it was Bob Dylan by the yard, and it was great.

'Disease Of Conceit' was Dylan distraught at the lack of faith, lack of belief... lack of anything. Conceit was a disease, he suggests, which turns the best into the worst, and Dylan was still capable of translating base metal into gold.

'Shooting Star' wrapped it all up, a beguilingly gentle melody at odds with the bridge, which had Dylan reflecting on the finality of it all. The song spoke of things "slipping away", but what was so encouraging was that Dylan had never sounded more retentive and in control. You can rarely divide artists or movements neatly into decades, but *Oh Mercy* was buoyant, and Dylan's triumphant conclusion to the 1980s too conveniently timed to be ignored.

After spending way too long in the foothills looking up, at the end of 1989 Bob Dylan was back on the mountain looking down into the valley below.

UNDER THE RED SKY

RELEASED: SEPTEMBER 1990. CURRENT ISSUE: CBS 4671882

It was a busy time for Bob Dylan. He received the prestigious 'Commandeur Des Arts & Des Lettres' award from the French Culture Minister, Jack Lang. He was coming off the critical hosannas accorded to *Oh Mercy*. He had been touring nigh-on incessantly since 1988. He got to meet Michael Bolton...

As with so many phases of Dylan's career, it wasn't a Gemini split, more Uncertainty dominant. Dylan had seen his own career eclipsed by lesser talents and younger disciples. Never submitting to tour sponsorship, shucking the corporate, homogeneous face of rock 'n' roll in the 1990s, Dylan defiantly continued to plough his own solitary furrow.

Such defiance didn't exactly ensure continuity. In concert, Dylan veered from triumph to embarrassment, the same sort of path he was weaving on record. With the praise for *Oh Mercy* still ringing in his ears, Dylan settled down in January 1990 to begin recording his next album. *Under The Red Sky* was everything *Oh Mercy* wasn't – sloppily written songs, lazily performed and unimaginatively produced. Even the all-star cast boasted on the sleeve ('David Crosby, George Harrison,

Bruce Hornsby, Elton John, Al Kooper, Slash, Jimmie & Stevie Ray Vaughan, Don Was and More') couldn't stop this one having 'Dog' stamped all over it and writ large.

Under The Red Sky was just shoddy; on the heels of *Oh Mercy* it was derisory. The title track had a nursery rhyme charm – indeed, within a year, Dylan was to record a version of the nursery rhyme 'This Old Man' for a Disney album – but the remaining tracks on *Under The Red Sky* were, at best forgettable, at worst, humiliating. The first bridge of '2 x 2' ("How much poison did they inhale...?") was reminiscent of the menace which pervaded *Oh Mercy*, but otherwise, where before there had been certainty and sureness, here was confusion and indecision.

'TV Talkin' Song' was a limp rewrite of 1975's 'Black Diamond Bay', relocated to

Speakers' Corner, Hyde Park ("a place" Dylan helpfully informs the uninitiated, "where people talk").

Then there's 'Wiggle Wiggle': worse than anything Dylan has ever recorded? Maybe not that bad, but certainly up there, jostling for position in that particular part of hell, where the jukebox plays nothing but 'Joey' and 'Had A Dream About You Baby'. 'Wiggle Wiggle' was the one the critics jumped on, particularly the line "Wiggle wiggle wiggle like a bowl of soup", which was taken as proof positive that Dylan had lost it, definitely, permanently, irrevocably. It was hard to disagree – it is hard to reconcile such a line with the man who wrote 'Desolation Row'. Of course, you can't get Hamlet or 'Like A Rolling Stone' every time out of the traps, but 'Wiggle Wiggle'...

Al Kooper struggled to make 'Handy Dandy' sound like 'Like A Rolling Stone', and the album concluded dismally with the nursery rhyme frivolity of 'Cat's In The Well', one of Dylan's weakest sounding vocals before a band that sounded hopelessly at odds with the singer.

Under The Red Sky showed all the desperate intensity of a man who had watched lesser talents eclipse him and was determined to prove he still had it in him. He had, in fact, already proved it with *Oh Mercy*, but he alone seemed conspicuously unaware of the fact.

Which brings us to another constant in Dylan's career – the artist's own reluctance to separate the truly inspired from the thoroughly mediocre. In Dylan's eyes, it seems as though 'Wiggle Wiggle' is as good a song as 'Mr Tambourine Man'. It must be galling to be Bob Dylan, and to be constantly, endlessly reminded of just how great you once were. For a songwriter – especially a songwriter so often touched by the hand of God as Bob Dylan – must look forward, and not keep looking back. But that doesn't stop 'Mr Tambourine Man' being a wonderful song.

Nothing can have the repercussions and ramifications of that song today. But then, there was a freshness and a verve to the music Dylan produced during the Sixties. No other person has created a body of songs like that, songs which were capable of such an impact. When you have singlehandedly redefined pop music by the time you are 24, you must need something else to keep you going at 54.

It is impossible to imagine, or re-create the impact of Dylan's music during the Sixties. In the faceless, heartless Nineties, you can get information from all around the world about anything at the flick of a switch, but the sense of solidarity, of community, of the world as a Global Village seems more remote than ever. There are too many distractions today. Nothing can ever match that impact.

Dylan understandably finds it galling to have his every effort as a writer stacked up against something he created 30 years before. But he must know, deep down, that an album like *Under The Red Sky* simply doesn't hold a candle to a sustained work such as *Highway 61 Revisited*. What we are grateful for is *Highway 61 Revisited*. That is what will live on. Anything after *Blonde On Blonde* is a bonus. *Under The Red Sky* simply sells to completists, who file it next to *Dylan & The Dead*. "Cancel", like the man said, "and pass on".

GOOD AS I BEEN TO YOU

RELEASED: NOVEMBER 1992. CURRENT ISSUE: COL 4727102

Rootless and unsettled, Dylan was on the ropes again after *Under The Red Sky*. He toured incessantly, more like a hungry teenager out to establish a name rather than one of rock's few legitimate legends.

Touring became Dylan's rationale in dealing with a confused and confusing world. Here he was, edging 50, over half his life spent in the public eye, hailed and lauded, but still out there playing with scratch bands to half-empty halls and increasingly indifferent audiences. These weren't the purists who booed when Bob went electric all those years ago; these were diehard, devoted friends, who were increasingly baffled by their idol's direction. In concert, Dylan was capable of delivering heart-stoppingly moving solo versions of 'Girl From The North Country' or gutsy reworkings of 'It Takes A Lot To Laugh (It Takes A Train To Cry)'. But too often, Dylan deconstructed fondly remembered songs, as heartlessly as a dissecting surgeon, to the dismay of audiences, who just gave up bothering and drifted away.

Dylan was still capable of drawing a crowd, this was, after all, Bob Dylan! The Tambourine Man, the man who turned The Beatles on to marijuana. The Rolling Stone, who a-changed the times all those years ago. Commercially, though, Dylan was dying on his feet, the only consolation came when Bob tugged on his Boo Wilbury hood again, though the group's second album lacked the appeal of their début, largely because the loss of Roy Orbison overshadowed it.

The release of the box set retrospective *The Bootleg Series* in 1991 did much to restore Dylan's standing. With his follow up to *Under The Red Sky*, 1992's *Good As I Been To You*, Dylan cast his eye even further back.

Good As I Been To You was Dylan's real *Self Portrait*. A faded sepia snapshot of the music which had led Bob down the snaking highway from Minnesota to the world. This was Dylan 'unplugged', but then Bob Dylan was unplugged before the electricity was even switched on.

Recorded at home, *Good As I Been To You* is

one man and his guitar, telling tales as old as fire. These are songs steeped in the folk and blues tradition, songs which stretch back centuries.

Those looking for feet of clay claimed *Good As I Been To You* as further proof of Dylan's writer's block. But many, more open to Dylan's reluctance to be pigeonholed, found the album a refreshing recognition of earlier, inspirational sources.

'Frankie & Albert' is the original 1888 title of the murder ballad, better known to later generations as 'Frankie & Johnny' (Elvis even made one of his dreadful mid-60s movies about the gambler who was shot by the slighted Nellie Bly). All through the album, Dylan dives deep and knowledgeably into the well-spring of the folk tradition. Derided and mocked for years and latterly ignored completely, folk was at last coming back into vogue; its simplicity and directness a welcome and authentic alternative to the superficiality of Eighties pop. The popularity of MTV's *Unplugged* format saw bands hastening to establish credibility by ditching electricity. Bob of course had already been there long before.

'Arthur McBride' was popularised by Paul Brady, an artist Dylan is known to admire. The song stretches right back to the mid-19th Century – a press gang song which turns to the waste of war and the strength of camaraderie. 'Arthur McBride' is worth seeking out, if only to hear Dylan sing 'shillelagh' as well as the shanty-derived "a rock-and-a-roll". Dylan's fondness for Irish music had run alongside his whole career – The Clancy Brothers were making their mark on folk music in the early Sixties, just as Dylan was breaking into Greenwich Village. Dylan has cited Liam Clancy as the best ballad singer he'd ever heard, and his tribute to his UK audience in 1969 came with a performance of The McPeake Family's 'Will Ye Go Lassie Go' (aka 'Wild Mountain Thyme' or 'Purple Heather').

'Jim Jones' is more widely known as 'Botany Bay', an 18th Century broadside ballad, originating on the streets of London, about transportation to the criminal colony of Australia. 'Black Jack Davey' can be traced back to the execution of a gypsy by Scottish officials in 1624. It has endured as long as any song in the tradition, being familiar down the centuries as 'The Gypsy Laddie' and 'Seventeen Come Sunday'.

The album's stand-out track is Dylan's chilling rendition of Stephen Foster's 'Hard Times'. Foster, best known as the composer of some of the 19th Century's most familiar parlour ballads ('Jeannie With The Light Brown Hair', 'Beautiful

Dreamer') penned this darkest of songs just prior to his death, aged 37, with as few cents in his penurious pockets.

In the main, the blues were held in reserve for Dylan's next album, one of the few exceptions on *Good As I Been To You* being a version of Howlin' Wolf's 'Sittin' On Top Of The World', popularised by Cream, but here returned firmly to its acoustic roots.

'Diamond Joe' sounds like a close relation of the characters in Dylan's own 'Lily, Rosemary & The Jack Of Hearts', but in fact goes back to the popular Cowboy songs forged on the American frontier during the 1870s.

Dylan was a fond custodian of the folk tradition. He was famously scathing about Joan Baez still singing "all those songs about roses growing out of maidens' brains", but latterly, Dylan has acted as a one-man museum of American popular music.

'Canadee-I-O' dates from the mid-19th Century, another song of suffering in remote and unimaginable places. Folk songs were the great communicators in the days before mass literacy. Dylan's audacious return to the folk tradition served to remind listeners that there was life before MTV. That one man and his guitar truly can outweigh the world.

He had begun life as a troubadour, a singer who could flit from town to town, because all he needed to tell his tales was a guitar. As he sailed past 50, Dylan returned to the road, and to hard travelling. *Good As I Been To You* was a trawl through the bayous and bywaters of the American folk tradition and the sea lanes of the North Atlantic. It was Dylan, doggedly pursuing his own determination to preserve that tradition, but as a living, breathing, timely thing, not an ossified museum exhibit.

Dylan's voice sounded as gnarled and aged-in-oak as the songs he was singing. Slipping and sliding over the centuries, *Good As I Been To You* was a defiant kiss-off to those who thought that folk music began with Billy Bragg.

Even so, the sniggering that greeted the news that Bob Dylan of all people had recorded 'Froggie Went A-Courtin'' made it a difficult choice of vintage song to defend. But as Allan Jones pointed out, the final lines significantly run: "If you want any more, you can sing it yourself".

This is Dylan going his own way. Singing it himself, for himself. It is Bob Dylan singing 'Froggie Went A-Courtin''. Fine by me. You got a problem with that?

BOB DYLAN world gone wrong

WORLD GONE WRONG

RELEASED: NOVEMBER 1993. CURRENT ISSUE: COL 4748572

In October 1992, when Columbia Records bafflingly chose to celebrate Dylan's 30 years on the label – he had actually signed to the label in October 1961 and released his début album in America in March 1962 – *Good As I Been To You* was Bob Dylan's most recent album on the market.

As the world (Pearl Jam, Neil Young, George Harrison, John Mellencamp) gathered to pay tribute to Bob (*Bob Dylan: The 30th Anniversary Concert Celebration* COL 474002, August 1993), Bob came out to remind us just where it all began. Dylan opened his short set with 'Song To Woody', the sound of Bob bringing it all back home.

At Bill Clinton's 1992 inauguration it was REM's Michael Stipe who read Woody's 'This Land Is Your Land', but who was that hooded figure playing guitar on the steps of the Capitol? For much of the decade, Dylan had hidden beneath a hood. The press was full of stories concerning his increasingly bizarre behaviour – turning the lights way down low at concerts to thwart photographers; cycling to his own gigs; writing songs with Michael Bolton.

In his sleeve notes to *World Gone Wrong*, Dylan said that the Never Ending Tour had in fact ended in 1991 with the departure of guitarist GE Smith (even though he was the musical director at the 30th Anniversary event in 1992) but that there had been subsequently, among others, the Money Never Runs Out Tour, One Sad Cry Of Pity Tour and the Why Do You Look At Me So Strangely Tour. Dylan was just always out there.

Yet as Peter Kemp wrote of Kenneth Tynan: "For a decade or so (he was) genuinely distinguished, then settled for being merely conspicuous". In the Nineties, as during the 1980s, Dylan seemed to be finding it difficult dealing with the changing times.

Dylan wasn't writing a novel. Following *Hearts Of Fire*, he had given up on the movies after they had given up on him. He shrugged off the good reviews for *Oh Mercy*, despite the hosannas, he hadn't particularly relished producer Daniel Lanois' painstaking approach, and the partnership had not been renewed. He didn't seem to particularly relish the praise he attracted, nor the tributes paid to him by lesser, but better known talents. Hell, he wasn't even writing any songs.

World Gone Wrong drew from the well of *Good As I Been To You*. Here were songs made popular by, rather than about, Blind Willie McTell. The album owed its origins to such obscure pioneers and popularisers of the lost music as Frank Hutchison, The Mississippi Sheiks, Lonnie Chatman, Willie Brown, The New Lost City Ramblers and Doc Watson.

World Gone Wrong is an album even older than its singer. Whereas *Good As I Been To You* drew on the folk tradition, the songs of Europe which had changed in the hands of America, *World Gone Wrong* was bitterly and caustically bluesy. For Dylan, the blues were the authentically American musical voice. His first album drew heavily on the blues tradition. His first major New York gig had been supporting bluesman John Lee Hooker, and the

sleeves of his Sixties albums were dotted with the names of blues veterans.

It is no accident that Dylan entitled the album *World Gone Wrong*. Through his eyes, it was a world reeling from the lack of spiritual values, a world obsessed by the superficial, a world which failed to recognise what had been, and refused to accept what was to come. The only truth Dylan found was in the past, he seemed to identify with the veneration and authenticity of the blues, and of the old blues singers.

Flouting convention, again, Dylan and his guitar were all over a landscape inhabited by roving gamblers, faithless wives, weeping mothers... 'Stack A Lee' was the most familiar of the songs to initiates, largely due to Lloyd Price's pile-driving New Orleans hit of 1958 – The Clash also used a snatch of the vintage murder ballad on *London Calling*.

'Jack-A-Roe' was another of those ballads which were the 18th Century equivalent of TV soap operas. The version Dylan sings here is a variation on a regular theme of the broadside ballads – a young girl pining for her absent lover, disguises herself as a soldier (or sailor) and serves alongside her true love.

Dylan saved his best vocal performance for the album's final track, Doc Watson's 'Lone Pilgrim'. He sounds strangely warm and consoling in the tragic telling of a deathly tale. But death is not the end; release (and relief) waits on high.

The faults of *World Gone Wrong* lay in the similarity to its predecessor, though it was bleaker in tone than *Good As I Been To You*. It also marked Dylan's fourth release of the decade, and while his prolificity was to be welcomed, it seemed strange and sad that only one of his Nineties albums had contained original, contemporary material.

The release of *World Gone Wrong* went by largely unremarked. Dylan made little impact outside those who had diligently followed his every faltering step since the faraway 1960s.

His movements and his motives were shady: he turned up crooning the old Jo Stafford favourite from the Fifties, 'You Belong To Me' on the soundtrack of *Natural Born Killers*. He contributed 'Boogie Woogie Country Girl' to a Doc Pomus tribute album. He had the chilling experience of seeing one of his songs covered by Emerson, Lake & Palmer. He found that his second album

Freewheelin' was the most expensive and collectable rock record ever released. Owners of the ultra rare stereo version with the four original tracks ('Solid Road', 'Let Me Die In My Footsteps', 'Gamblin' Willie', 'Talkin' John Birch Society Blues') could expect to receive somewhere in excess of £10,000.

Perhaps strangest of all, in view of his own Luddite reluctance to come to terms with late 20th Century technology, Dylan found himself the subject of *Highway 61 Interactive*, a 12-hour CD-Rom program. While at the same time, with the other hand, he was busy suing Apple Computers for hijacking his surname as a program title.

The biggest controversy surrounding Dylan's name during the 1990s, came when he sanctioned the use of 'The Times They Are A-Changin'' for a television advert promoting accountants Coopers & Lybrand. Dylan wouldn't give permission for his original version, but even allowing Richie Havens' cover to be used, was a smack in the eye for many. It had long been an article of faith that Dylan kept the corporate Moloch at arm's length.

Dylan had never succumbed to tour sponsorship (Miller Lite Presents Bob 'Blowin' In

The Wind' Dylan In Concert), he had refused to let his back catalogue be tampered with, he doggedly went his own way, making music that sometimes only he believed in... And yet, he let one of the few genuine, *bona fide* anthems of the 1960s be used to promote a faceless financial institution. Even Coopers & Lybrand couldn't believe their luck: "The real coup is getting the author of change affiliated with our company".

Hadn't Dylan written somewhere about advertising "conning you" into believing? It can't have been for the cash (covers of Dylan songs by top-selling acts such as Guns n' Roses and the licensing of his compositions for film soundtracks already ensured a very healthy income). It seemed like the ultimate sell out, from the one man who was still perceived as being capable of holding the moral high ground.

Still those 1960s just wouldn't go away; they came back home again at Woodstock '94. The enduring myth of Woodstock '69 had seen it venerated as the festival. It didn't have the best line up, it wasn't the best-attended, it wasn't the only festival filmed, but something about Woodstock rang down the years.

Controversy hounded the 25th anniversary re-run of the original festival. First time around, it had begun life as a tribute to the man who shunned it, but typically, he came back to it a quarter of a century later.

In an age when The Eagles could charge $120 a ticket for a reunion tour, the ticket prices for Woodstock '94 shouldn't have come as too much of a surprise. They did. It was like charging admission to church. But that didn't stop an estimated 300,000 turning out – to the real Woodstock this time around – the 1969 original had been held at nearby Bethel.

Dylan was one of the unexpected triumphs of the festival, back on a roll as far as his live work was concerned. When he hit New York in the autumn of 1994, he was joined onstage by long-time admirers Bruce Springsteen and Neil Young for rowdy encores of 'Rainy Day Women...' and 'Highway 61 Revisited'.

Dylan's rollercoaster years were over, for the time being. In concert, he was performing with a zeal he hadn't mustered in years. His writer's block may have remained intact, but he has shown himself more than capable of commemorating, even celebrating, a past which at times had threatened to drag him down. In many ways, Dylan seemed to have come full circle and was now as buoyant as at any time during the decade.

Following the likes of Eric Clapton, Mariah Carey, Nirvana, Bruce Springsteen and Tony Bennett, Bob Dylan finally came to MTV to record his own *Unplugged* album.

UNPLUGGED

RELEASED: APRIL 1995. CURRENT ISSUE: COL 4783742

As a format, *Unplugged* was already showing cracks – the plugs were all the way in for Springsteen's set, and Plant & Page had cranked the amps all the way up to 11. Late in 1994 though, Dylan – surrounded by a disreputable looking bunch of *hombres* – sat down and delivered his best live album ever.

Dylan's selection of material was as impeccable as his choice of shirt. 'With God On Our Side' and 'The Times They Are A-Changin'' are all-embracing and wise; 'Desolation Row', desiccated but nonetheless awesome. For the first time in ages, Dylan sang the anthems with fervour, and in a voice as gravelly as Monument Valley. These are songs from a time before MTV, of a time almost before TV.

Even the sluggish 'John Brown', an anti-war song from 1963, was treated with an intensity and commitment Dylan hadn't mustered in ages. The obvious crowd-pleasers – 'Rainy Day Women' and 'Knockin' On Heaven's Door' – were compensated by the inclusion of jokers in the pack like 'Shooting Star' and 'Desolation Row'. Close up, Dylan had a tendency to pull his lips back over his teeth, like a fox salivating over prey. 'Like A Rolling Stone' became a slow,

stately voyage through perhaps his best-loved song. And he asks us "How does it feel?" And we answer, equally mysteriously, "How does it feel?"

Bob even took a guitar solo, knees bent, crouching in appropriately heroic pose. Yet now, there was nothing comic in the pose, rather something genuinely heroic about the figure on display.

The show was paced, songs rose and fell, as if Dylan had learned something about performance from all those years of footslogging. Dylan's *Unplugged* lives and breathes vivacity. A journal of rediscovery. Dylan's vocals are breathless and urgent, but there is a playfulness in his phrasing and delivery, He injects nuance into his performance. It isn't as if he's trapped in the quicksand of a time long gone, 'Dignity' and 'Shooting Star' sit as easily in performance as any other vintage.

The flaws are in the needless truncation of 'Tombstone Blues', 'Desolation Row' and 'With God On Our Side'. If these Sixties' "word-fests" just eat up Dylan's memory, he should ditch them. But then his most recent song, 'Dignity', is as verse-crazy as anything he's written.

The show ends with 'Like A Rolling Stone'. Dylan smiles as he fumbles the intro. He even admits that maybe the instruments weren't in tune and the intro could do with improving. Now there's a first. Going up to the top, the song eventually winds down, deflating, like air coming out of a leaking Lilo, and it's over, and he quits the stage, to the sound of whoops and applause. It's a sound he's familiar with.

For the first time in maybe a decade, it's as if Bob Dylan himself understands what we have known all along: that, hey, these are unmatchable songs. There is something special about this material. There is greatness afoot.

That momentum carried Dylan into Europe in the spring of 1995. It was a Greatest Hits package, but one which shifted around 60 per cent of the set each night. Few other acts of that stature would have the audacity to change things around that much; but then few other acts have a back

catalogue to draw on which could sustain such a move.

Onstage, Dylan was transformed. He and the band were playing the same song, at the same time. Somewhere, Dylan had taken lessons in phrasing, enunciation, pacing. There was magic in the air, even 'Joey' – out of nearly 1000 original titles, my least favourite Bob Dylan song ever – was worth listening to. For heaven's sake, even Dylan's harmonica-playing was worth hearing.

Any residual doubts were dispelled with his performance of 'Mr Tambourine Man'. I know I wasn't the only man with a beard who cried a silent tear when they heard Dylan's arresting and devotional version of one of his greatest-ever songs.

'The Times They Are A-Changin'' could, by 1995, have come across as little more than karaoke protest, but Dylan's handling did much to lend it dignity. In this performance, as in so many other treatments on those magic nights, the composer himself seemed to have become aware of just how much these songs mean to his audience. How important those songs were to the lives of everyone in that room.

Bob Dylan, Brixton Academy, March 1995. God-like. Bob knows where he goes next.

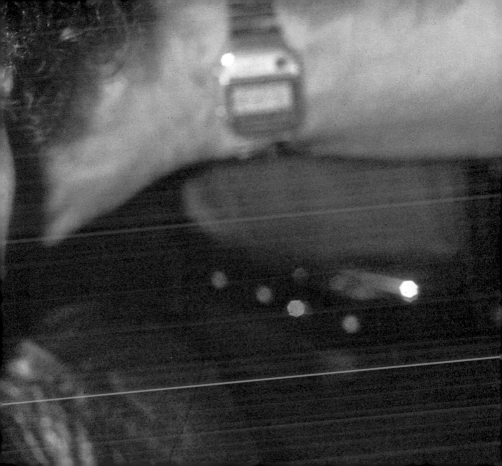

COMPILATIONS

Dylan has made bewildering and diverse guest appearances on albums ranging from Harry Belafonte at the very beginning, through 'new Dylan' Steve Goodman to U2. He has contributed to live souvenir albums of The Woody Guthrie Memorial Concert, 1968; Bangladesh, 1971; The Last Waltz, 1976; his own 30th Anniversary Tribute, 1992 and Woodstock '94.

His relationship with his record label, Columbia, has been fractious. But then, Dylan has never been the easiest of clients – recording some of pop's most wondrous, weaving music, then refusing to release it! His record sales are a fraction of labelmates Simon & Garfunkel or George Michael. His impact, though, remains unmatched and undeniable.

It was only in 1975 that Dylan and his label recognised he had a past, with the official release of *The Basement Tapes*. Ten years later, *Biograph* set the pace for box sets, which was fully realised in 1992 with the release of *The Bootleg Series*. Dylan is one of rock's most bootlegged artists, but unlike, say

Led Zeppelin or The Rolling Stones, whose bootleg repertoire is largely culled from live performance over the years, much of Dylan's reputation rests on one-off, unreleased studio performances.

There is also an astonishing backlog of live tapes which have never officially seen the light of day, but few people, Dylan included, have the patience to wade through 1,100 live versions of 'Like A Rolling Stone' and sift out the definitive performance.

In the meantime, here is what has been officially issued to commemorate the one and only...

BOB DYLAN GREATEST HITS

RELEASED: MARCH 1967. CURRENT ISSUE: CBS 450882

Today, a three-year delay between albums is unremarkable, even commonplace. Back then, the fact that Bob Dylan hadn't had any 'fresh product' on the market since the release of *Blonde On Blonde* six months before, threw his label into nervous panic, and they released this workmanlike hits collection to fill the gap. The only real incentive for fans was 'Positively 4th Street' included for the first time on an album. One of Dylan's bitterest put-downs, the song's spite hasn't diminished down the years. Speculation has persisted over the identity of the victim – Phil Ochs is the hapless favourite.

Bob Dylan Greatest Hits only scratched the surface of the Dylan canon. It did, however, show what a long, strange trip it had been from the quiet protest of 'Blowin' In The Wind' to the hazy turbulence of 'I Want You'. And all in four years.

For many years, this has remained the Dylan hits package. It badly needs overhauling, amalgamating Greatest Hits I, II and III into a comprehensive package for today's CD-owners. The burgeoning market demands one, catch-all, 75-minute Greatest Hits disc to reach the mass audience – *The Beautiful South's Greatest Hits*, for example, outsold The Beatles and Stone Roses at Christmas 1994.

BOB DYLAN'S GREATEST HITS 2

RELEASED: 1967. CURRENT ISSUE: COL 4712432

A European release, to cash in on Bob Dylan, Pop Star. It duplicates three tracks from the original 1967 *Greatest Hits* ('I Want You', 'Rainy Day Women...', 'Just Like A Woman'). Nervous at the lack of a new album, six tracks are also lifted straight off *Blonde On Blonde*, while the remainder are an arbitrary selection – 'It Takes A Lot To Laugh...', 'Just Like Tom Thumb's Blues', 'Chimes Of Freedom', 'Gates Of Eden'. The album was made widely available in the UK on CD in 1993.

MORE BOB DYLAN GREATEST HITS

RELEASED: NOVEMBER 1971. CURRENT ISSUE: CDCBS 67239

For such a reclusive figure, and one so reluctant to release any new material, 1971 saw Dylan's profile as high as at any time during his career. His only novel, *Tarantula*, begun on the road during the chaos of the mid-Sixties, was finally published to a respectful, if baffled, response. Dylan was also the high point of George Harrison's Bangla Desh benefit concert at Madison Square Garden that August.

Coming in the lull between *New Morning* and *Pat Garrett & Billy The Kid*, the incentive to buy *More Bob Dylan Greatest Hits* was the five new tracks hidden away at the end of the double album. Space was not found, though, for Dylan's single-only release of 1971 'George Jackson', although his other non-album song of the same year – 'Watching The River Flow' – opened this set. Dylan supervised the selection of this collection, and it certainly did offer a broader perspective of his work, including 'Lay

Lady Lay', his only legitimate 'hit' since his mid-Sixties peak.

Given Dylan's involvement, it was a surprise to find the *Self Portrait* version of 'The Mighty Quinn' instead of its 'Basement Tape' original, especially as three other 'basement' songs ('I Shall Be Released', 'You Ain't Goin' Nowhere' and 'Down In The Flood') had made their way overground and onto this album. They weren't actually from the legendary 1967 sessions at Big Pink, but from a more recent session Dylan had held with folk veteran Happy Traum. 'You Ain't Goin' Nowhere', familiar from The Byrds' landmark 1968 *Sweetheart Of The Rodeo* was even rewritten to include a reference to the group's leader Roger McGuinn. The haunting 'I Shall Be Released' was taken at a breezy, singalong pitch here, while 'Down In The Flood' lacked the sense of mystery evident on bootlegs.

One of the other new songs, 'When I Paint My Masterpiece' had appeared on The Band's fourth album *Cahoots*, earlier in the year – although Dylan's own version missed out the splendid bridge "Sailin' round the world in a dirty gondola/Oh to be back in the land of Coca Cola". But the outstanding addition was a beautiful song, 'Tomorrow Is A Long Time'. Written in 1962 for long-time girlfriend Suze Rotolo (familiar from the cover of *Freewheelin'*), it was taken from a 1963 New York concert recorded by Dylan's label for release as his first official live album, but which had never surfaced. It is Dylan's finest song of lost love; it is one of the best ever songs about parting and it is one of only two Bob Dylan songs ever recorded by Elvis Presley (Elvis also cut 'Don't Think Twice, It's Alright' in 1971). Inexplicably, Elvis covered the song (which in 1969, Dylan called his favourite cover version) for inclusion on the soundtrack of the 1966 stinker *Spinout*. Elvis takes it at a slightly country pace, a sensitive version of a haunting song, uncomfortably sitting alongside mere soundtrack fillers such as 'Smorgasbord' and 'Beach Shack'.

BIOGRAPH

RELEASED: NOVEMBER 1985. CURRENT ISSUE: CDCBS 66509

There had, of course, been rumours, whispers. *Biograph* was reluctantly released ("All it is, really" Dylan candidly admitted,

"is repackaging, and it'll cost a lot of money"). There were 18 unreleased songs or performances sprinkled over a total of 53 songs. In the past, the few box sets there had been were opportunities to package up just the hits; *Biograph* altered that, and paved the way for record companies to rifle systematically through their vaults to enhance an already established artist's stature by boxing them up for posterity.

For all the faults in its selection, and Dylan's reluctance to endorse wholeheartedly 'all new' old material, *Biograph* is worthy of attention because of the comprehensive picture it paints of Dylan's growth and breadth, the unreleased material and the two lengthy booklets, which offer the fullest and frankest evidence of Dylan discussing his own songs in detail.

Biograph was welcomed, offering the opportunity to replace warped and scratched vinyl bootlegs with pristine, first generation masters.

'I'll Keep It With Mine' was one of those heartfelt, mysterious songs which Dylan seemed to be able to pluck out of the air at will. Addressed to a spectral, wraith-like female (Nico? Judy Collins?) it sounds like it means a lot more than it actually does. 'Mixed Up

Confusion' the first single, which, had it been more widely available, would have obviated a lot of the flak which accompanied the electric period of 1965/66, was a raucous, Little Richard-led rocker, celebrating Bob's childhood love of piano-pounding rock 'n' roll.

'Percy's Song' was a lyrical, wistful reflection on wrongful imprisonment and lost friendship. It was beautifully covered by Sandy Denny and Fairport Convention in 1969. 'Lay Down Your Weary Tune' stands as one of Dylan's finest ever songs: a musician's response to God, the universe and the clanging, resurgent power of nature. An elemental song, hard to credit Dylan's youth when he composed it. It sounds older than time, sung by a boy before his first beard.

Aside from 'Just Like Tom Thumb's Blues', which surfaced on the B-side of 'I Want You' in 1966, there had, inexplicably, been no official souvenirs of Dylan's 1966 tour with The Band. *Biograph* at least partially redressed the balance – haunting, first-half solo versions of 'Visions Of Johanna' and 'It's All Over Now Baby Blue' were included, while a searing, chaotic 'I Don't Believe You' hinted at the electric power which

had been regularly mustered every night.

Equally baffling was the delayed release of the wonderful 'Abandoned Love', which had been excluded from *Desire* in favour of 'Joey'. Other odd, revealing fragments surfaced – 'Jet Pilot' was a palimpsest for 'Tombstone Blues', an alternative 'You're A Big Girl Now' was more mellow; 'Forever Young', a snatched and enticing moment.

If proof was required that Dylan's star hadn't dimmed since the passing of the Sixties, 1981's 'Caribbean Winds' provided it. 'Up To Me' was Dylan in rare confessional mood, a solo troubadour, playing for another of those mystery women who fluttered around his muse, moths to the flame.

Biograph is too random, its juxtaposition of tracks seems unhappily muddled on record. Fans would already have the official versions of, say, 'Mr Tambourine Man' twice before, while less devoted followers wanting only the 'pop Bob' of 'Lay Lady Lay', would be baffled by the strung out melancholy of 'Visions Of Johanna'. But flawed as it was, at least it was a beginning in the tracing of what had been.

THE BOOTLEG SERIES, VOLS 1-3

RELEASED: MARCH 1991. CURRENT ISSUE: COL 4680862

Of all the great 'lost' Bob Dylan songs, the most lost was 'Farewell Angelina'. Even those doorstop-size Dylan directories which dutifully annotated his every bowel movement, failed to confirm that he had actually recorded the song, familiar to many from Joan Baez's version. Recorded during that incredibly fertile year of 1965, 'Farewell Angelina' was the Holy Grail for all Dylan collectors. And here it was, Disc 2, Track 5. And, of course, after a quarter of a century, it wasn't that great a version of a song so legendary that the actuality could only be a disappointment.

If *Biograph* had dipped a toe in the water, *The Bootleg Series* was a full-scale immersion, 58 never-before-released songs spread over four hours, with John Bauldie's song-by-song commentary putting it all in some sort of wondrous context.

The Bootleg Series rapped through Dylan's 30-year career at a lickspittle pace. Here was the fledgling Woody, the bard of protest, the folk-rock monarch, the shadowy Woodstock resident, the soul-bearer, the gospel proselytiser and, ultimately, the mysterious and irreplaceable Bob Dylan.

It was an enticing package, a jemmy to the door of Pharaoh's tomb. Until now, we had officially glimpsed Dylan through a glass, darkly – snatches of poorly-recorded, haphazardly chronological bootlegs. Here was all the glory, from the first impressions of a hostile city on 'Hard Times In New York Town' to the culmination of the piledriving 1989 'Series Of Dreams'.

Familiar titles abounded :'Let Me Die In My Footsteps', 'Rambling, Gambling Willie', 'Eternal Circle', 'Walkin' Down The Line', 'Mama You Been On My Mind', 'Sitting On A Barbed Wire Fence', 'Blind Willie McTell'... Then there were the new, unheard mysteries – an acoustic 'Subterranean Homesick Blues', 'Like A Rolling Stone' in waltz time! The not-even-rumoured 'Santa Fe' from the basement tapes, the mysterious, missing *Blood On The Tracks* out-takes, an 'Every Grain Of Sand' demo with howling dog on chorus...

It was inconceivable that any other act could compile such a selection as *The Bootleg Series*. The sheer scope, the quality and quantity of the material is astonishing. Dylan's deft acoustic guitar picking is given full rein on 'Worried Blues', the breadth of his singing finding full voice on 'No More Auction Block' (buried inside which is the melody for his own 'Blowin' In The Wind'). Dylan had never sounded older nor wiser. He was barely 20 at the time of this recording.

The Bootleg Series demonstrated just how far Dylan had come, and how all-embracing his influence was – a strong case can be made for 'Subterranean Homesick Blues' and 'Last Thoughts On Woody Guthrie' as white rap. It provided a revealing fly-on-the-wall account of how 'I'll Keep It With Mine' weaved with a band, and almost ended up on *Blonde On Blonde*.

And all the while, there were the pictures (page 29 of the booklet and on the back of the three CD cases) of tapes - piles and piles of boxes, miles and miles of tapes – like Dylan is saying, "You ain't heard nothin' yet!" And the picture on the cover of the booklet, Bob's driving licence, with his own side-splitting, birthday-altering birth date (You could hear the astrologers moan: "But he was always a Gemini...")

It was a kaleidoscope of Bob Dylans – the fervent speaker-out against indignity and champion of the underdog ('Walls Of Red Wing', 'Who Killed Davey Moore?', 'Only A Hobo'); then the surge of electricity through the words, hurling you into the unimagined worlds of 'She's Your Lover Now'.

The early songs display Dylan's mastery of the folk tradition, his ability as an interpretative singer ('Kingsport Town', 'Moonshiner') and his agility at writing in the traditional, border ballad style ('Seven Curses').

Here was Dylan all over the place, but coming back to a remarkably controlled centre. A man fumbling, but ultimately in control of his art and his destiny. Releasing *The Bootleg Series*, Bob Dylan shifted the focus from the future to the past, and garnered some of the best reviews of his entire career. Some critics carped at the failure of the box set to fully represent Dylan's unreleased *ouevre,* but the majority settled for the pleasure of hearing pristine, first generation master copies of songs they thought they'd never live to hear on disc. It was a testimony to a unique talent, a testament to what had been.

BOB DYLAN'S GREATEST HITS VOLUME 3

RELEASED: NOVEMBER 1994: COL 4778052

Trying to bring Dylan to the attention of the CD-buying audience of the Nineties, his record label again tried to convert the indifferent mass market into purchasers. The title almost left room for legal action – only 'Knockin' On Heaven's Door' was a bona-fide hit. By no stretch of the imagination could the 11-minute 'Brownsville Girl' or nursery rhyme 'Under The Red Sky' be termed 'hits'.

The necessary incentive for those who had everything anyway, was the inclusion of the contradictory "brand new Dylan classic" 'Dignity'. 'Dignity' was a rollicking, rockabilly chunk sliced off the *Oh Mercy* sessions and re-produced. It confirmed Dylan's inability to pronounce the word 'mirror', and – a first for Bob this – namechecked a member of the British royal family.

Otherwise, Volume 3 was a satisfactory treading water exercise. It offered the opportunity to re-appraise Dylan's work from that most lost of decades, the Eighties. By hearing 'Jokerman', 'Brownsville Girl', 'Ring Them Bells' and 'Series Of Dreams' together on one album, sitting alongside such Seventies' stalwarts as 'Changing Of The Guards' and 'Tangled Up In Blue', you were struck again by the sheer ability and intelligence at work.

If the album had come from Jeff Buckley, it would have been hailed. As it was Bob Dylan, it was widely ignored, not troubling the chart statisticians either here or in America.

Of course there were worries, this was after all the fourth release on the trot of cover versions, vintage material or previously available songs. Aside from *Under The Red Sky*, Dylan hadn't released an album of original material all decade, but when the material he was releasing was as good as *The Bootleg Series* or 'Dignity', such worries could surely be cast aside.

One of the problems with Bob Dylan, of course, is the Bob Dylan he drags around with him. As a young man, he irrevocably altered the face, not only of popular music, but of popular culture. He injected literacy and commitment

into pop music, he re-wrote the rule book, and on the way, provided pop with some of its most searing, inimitable and satisfactory moments.

As he uncomfortably keeps on, dogged by a past which is mercifully commemorated on tape, vinyl and film, Dylan remains determined not to be shackled by that past which everyone else finds so exhilarating and liberating. For Dylan, that past is stifling.

He has liberated us with a body of work unequalled in pop. He deserves to live as he wants. He has given so much already. Of course it's a rough and rocky road ahead; with the prospect of a new Bob Dylan album which could take you anywhere – the long-cherished album of instrumental music, cover versions of 40s standards, Bob Dylan & The Mormon Tabernacle Choir... who knows?

In the meantime, the notorious 1966 "Judas" concert will finally see an official release, nearly 30 years after the legendary tour with The Band. Equally certain is that after all these years, Bob Dylan still lives the life of a hard travelling Wilbury rather than a dilettante mega star. He alone knows what keeps him up there, let's just hope that whatever it is keeps him going.

12/99 (35940)